Celebrating

60

Celebrating

60

Impulsive meditations on more than six decades.

Publisher: Prairie Wind Writing Centre
Millet, Alberta

ISBN # 978-1-894045-03-2

Dedication

To Mom and Dad,
who gave me life,
hope, and a moral compass

and

to Tom and Nels,
my cherished brothers.

Acknowledgements

I am grateful for the hours of listening that Allen so graciously endured and for the support that he never failed to provide. I am indebted to Ella, Sharon, and Susan for reading and commenting on the initial manuscript. Thank you to Jaklin, Fern, and Terry for their editorial comments. Thank you Sandi and Lynda for helping me fulfill a life-long yearning. I am grateful to the village of my upbringing for the experience of community that was so core to the development of my own voice. A special thanks to Hal.

Table of Contents

The privilege of a life time is to become who you really are.

Carl Jung

Prologue

The words of Alberta Einstein, "Is there not a certain satisfaction in the fact that natural limits are set to the life of an individual, so that at its conclusion it may appear as a work of art?"[1] are an invitation to wonder about that tapestry of our own lives.

During my sixtieth year, I wrote a series of essays reflecting on my first six decades using the lens of gratitude. The process of doing so was an opportunity to reflect on the threads of my life woven into the being of who I am. The seventh decade is now fast approaching.

For reasons not fully clear to me, I am now willing to make public what previously has been a private reflection. Perhaps with each passing year of life I concern myself less and less about what someone else may think. Life is increasingly about living the values I have come to hold. I do so with varying consistency and intensity but I no longer flounder about the essential issues.

I share these essays with neither humility nor confidence of their relevance to others. They are, however, an invitation to reflect on your own journey.

Each essay is an honest conversation with myself. After hours of tinkering with the hopes of updating certain facts and perspectives, my choice is to have the document remain as it was written at the turn of the decade.

1   Einstein: *A Portrait.* (1984). Corte Madera, CA:Pomegranate Artbooks. p.118.

Preparing for celebration:
Laying the table

Life is the cumulative effect of a handful of
significant shocks.[2]

Nassim Taleb

---

2   Taleb, nassim Nicholas, (2007). *The Black Swan,* New York:
Random House, p.xix.

Celebrations take preparation. In the Scandinavian tradition, the laying of the table is an art form. The guest is welcomed to an ambiance that accompanies a feast. Things match. Colors are tasteful, although likely conservative. Understatement rather than overstatement is the tone. Quality will simply be there in the polished silver, the single flower, and the cloth napkins. Each aspect may have a story. It may be Aunt Ellen's silver except for the candlesticks that were a wedding present. The flower will be freshly picked from the garden. An elderly friend may have embroidered the napkins, and the dinnerware has likely hosted decades of family events.

Life is, in some, way a celebration in the making. I am not sure that I noticed the metaphor until recently.

I was setting the stage for what would be "my year", a sort of laying the table for celebration. It would be my year to pamper myself with travel, short courses, and special events. My year never happened. Early in January of "my" year, Allen was diagnosed with an aggressive lymphoma that would be the focus of our entire year. Combined with the financial crash of 2008, I was well positioned to whine during my sixtieth year. Focusing on celebration seemed a potential antidote.

As I entered my seventh decade there were, of course, six previous decades. There have been many feasts and much spilled milk. A decade by decade review of the highlights is the backdrop to the essays. My recollection of those years is solely mine. From among the endless memories only a few come forward spontaneously. This book was not intended to be autobiographical. Rather, I set myself the task of generating reflective essays, the focus of which was to be the decades lived and, to a lesser degree, the decades-in-waiting.

I will forego the common practice of apologizing for writing about one's own life. It's the only life I have lived, and it is therefore, the only one with which I am intimately acquainted. I make no apologies for it and have no regrets about how it has unfolded. Then and now, I am truly grateful for my life, and I have intentionally chosen to focus on aspects of life that, to me, feel worthy of celebration. In so doing, I recognize that events present themselves to us in a distorted way. My views are not to be privileged as truth nor do they imply greater insight into events than others who shared the encounters I report.

The first of my six decades passed without remarkable incidents. I was raised on a farm, the youngest of three, with two older brothers. Tom, the eldest, was diagnosed as a brittle diabetic at age two. As siblings, Nels and I were constantly aware that low blood sugars were dangerous for Tom. There were no sugarcoated cereals in our household, and the nurse from the health care unit instructed us on how to inject insulin should the need arise. We practiced on oranges.

The nearest girl lived a mile away. We were though, very different. She didn't ride horseback, and I didn't share her love of books. I did visit and have lemonade on occasion but there were no adventures with this peer. She was an unexpected child of older parents who were notably overly protective. The next girl was five miles away so visits were infrequent. Her family was Catholic. Our family was of the Lutheran tradition. That reality, and the fact we were in different school districts, added to the unlikelihood that we would meet socially.

As virtually the only daughter in a community of sons, I formed a special relationship with the adult women, many of whom I recall fondly. I had an Aunt Millie who lived a mile away and welcomed my unannounced arrivals. Those were in the days when a child could safely head off on their own down a country road to the neighbors. She had four sons so I was a valued visitor. It never entered my mind that I wasn't.

Time by myself was common and to this day, welcome. Dolls were of no interest despite my mother's labor of love to provide home made special outfits for my one and only doll. I could play ball with the best of the boys and shoot a pellet gun somewhat better. I played a better than average game of checkers, could bake brownies on my own by eight, and insisted on a hockey stick when my brothers got one. Tuesdays were special. That was the day my dad bought hogs in Wetaskiwin for the Livestock Co-op. Occasionally I would spend the whole day with him. On days when I wasn't with him, he never forgot to bring a O'Henry bar home for Nels and I. Tom got peanuts.

School was easy for me. My first camera was acknowledgment for placing first in class in grade four. That was my first year in the centralized school. Until then, we had attended a one room rural school. And yes, someone had to break the ice on the wash basin, and we were obliged to take a cod liver oil pill every day! And yes, at times, we did ride horseback to school.

I can't recall turning ten. My birthday is in late November so there was likely a skating party or a sleep over. Early in my second decade I was catapulted into maturity by meeting death face to face.

Claude, a young Welsh man of twenty-two, had become part of our family for eight months. On a rainy April 1, 1960, he was clearing trees from a pasture several miles from the farmstead. An innocent walk to call him for supper left a lifetime imprint. While Dad joined the neighbors for coffee, Tom and I jogged the muddy last mile. Claude's body was already blue when Tom and I found him. The Ferguson tractor had flipped, crushing him during his attempted jump to safety. He lay face down in the soil that he had been helping to break. Inexperienced, he had pulled a log up a small incline with too long a rope. In an instant, his life was gone and mine was changed forever.

Tom left first. He directed me to stay at the site. He would run for help. Initially, I squatted by Claude's body. I remember thinking, "This is what death looks like. He is blue. I think he is dead if he is blue." I recall the blood on his left visible ear. It wasn't long before I followed Tom's example and left the scene for help. My logic was that Tom might get low blood sugars on his way.

An unintended veil of silence settled over the death. To this day no one has ever spoken to me of that event except Claude's own mother, who I met in Wales fifteen years later.

Claude, the only son of a wealthy Welsh widow, had come to Canada at twenty-one, simply exploring as young men do. At twenty-two, he was dead. He had connected with our family through the local Agricultural College and what was intended to be a stay of weeks had melded into a stay of months and a new direction for his life.

After his death, I corresponded with his mother for years, finally visiting her in 1975. I slept in Claude's room. In his room there were only two photos - his and mine.

In 1964, I encountered the reality of mortality once again. I was fifteen. There had been many a hot chocolate and crib game on Sunday afternoons in Freeman and Val's home. Freeman taught me to play crib and my only "29" hand was in a game with him. He was the choir director. Although far from a skilled musician, I was the choir pianist. At 46, it took him nine weeks to die of nephritis. His advice and our talks during those weeks were formative in my development.

In 1966, Chris, Milly and Lars' son, died. He was our childhood friend, the kid of Grant McEwan stories. With a crop of red hair, a personality of Denis the Menace, and a willingness to try anything, we did what kids do. We rode our horses like Ben Hur, blew out candles together at each other's birthdays, fell off homemade rafts and built more than one tree house together.

In the early hours of dawn, at 19, he went through the windshield of his vehicle having fallen asleep at the wheel. Seat belts were not mandatory in those days. A strange turn of events placed me in the situation of having to inform his parents of his demise. It was that, or let the Royal Canadian Mounted Police do so. I couldn't do that to Milly and Lars. They were visiting Jasper where I was working for the summer. I will never forget Milly sitting on the edge of the Bed and Breakfast bed that I had directed them to and saying, "I have had such a lovely day, and all day my son has been dead." I was learning life was unpredictable, perhaps even fragile. Death didn't necessarily announce itself.

I have no recollection of turning twenty. I was,

by then, married to a charming Norwegian, running a home, teaching school, and within one course of completing my Bachelors' of Education degree. I had crammed all but one course of a four-year program into three years and was off to the job market with gusto, prepared to support a new husband's aspiration to attend university.

My twenties were in retrospect rather turbulent. The sequence went approximately like this. A couple of years of teaching. Graduate school in Educational Foundations. Divorce. Or was it abandonment? After agreeing to a year of separation I was, even in my youth, wise enough to recognize that I needed to either be "in" a marriage, or "out" of the marriage. When my husband returned one year to the day still undecided, I decided on "out". After court, presided over by a puzzled judge, we bought cross-country skis together. Lars returned to his pursuit of Shangri La and the ideal wife. To my knowledge, he remains single. During the first summer of my freedom, I drove my 1966 pink Pontiac Parisienne to Mexico and back, enjoying anonymity and ensuring my safety by camping each evening near the biggest family with the largest dog.

Glen entered my life in my twenties. He remains in my heart today. He was 36 years my senior with the body of a man half his age. We canoed Alberta rivers, hiked England, cycled France, and took courses together. I supported his dream of a hobby farm upon retirement while he encouraged my pursuit of a doctorate. In deciding that the age difference would become an issue over time, perhaps logic failed us both. Transforming the relationship to a friendship was painful. He went on to volunteer in Alaska, to travel to India, to ocean kayak at seventy-five, and at seventy-nine, to hike the West Coast Trail, well known for being a challenging feat. At eighty, his heart began a decline that ended his life at eighty-six. To this day, I miss his letters. Once he moved to the coast, we would alternately choose a book that we would both read and discuss it in our letters. The last one we shared was *The Culture of Hope*. Neither of us cared for Margaret Atwood. After *Alias Grace*, we gave up on Atwood.

Romance wounded me a second time when I was charmed by an Arkansas psychiatrist at a weeklong workshop. Six months later, I was on my way to a new life. I visited Little Rock. He came to Canada to meet my family. The hellos and goodbyes had been said. Having given up my apartment, resigned my job, and sold my car, the 5:00 a.m. call from him saying, "Don't come. I can't handle it" was among those experiences in life that simply eludes words. We never spoke again. His buddy, another psychiatrist whom I had met when I was in Arkansas, called me several days later. I recall his exact words. "Ronna, the only thing I can figure out is that what he most wants and what he is most afraid of come in the same package." I was left to heal on my own. Thankfully, my job was mine again if I wanted it. I wanted it!

The last half of my twenties saw the onset of a life threatening illness. It crept in slowly. It took me to the edge of death. At five feet seven inches, I was 88 pounds when I was flown to Mayo for life saving surgery. Thanks to a mother who insisted that no one in the family was to die before her, a father who cared, and friends whose love was endless, I became one of what science now calls "the black swans". We are anomalies. We don't fit. We don't die on time. We beat the odds and bother the world of health care sciences because we make prognostication only an art. I was not symptom free but I would live.

Five months after my surgery, at ninety-nine pounds, I successfully defended my dissertation. As I entered the examination room, I felt a calmness that I had not anticipated. Having been to hell and back in the previous months of illness, the next hours were not scary. Not long into the oral defense, the six men who sat around that boardroom table, and in those days it was always men, knew it was over. After entering an operating room months prior not knowing if I would come out alive, there wasn't an academic question that was frightening. The little tinge of curiosity I harbored about whether they had been easy on me in the exam process, given my illness, was put to rest when my research won a national award months later. I often said "I know who went to Mayo. I don't know who came home." It is no small gift to be given one's life back. Who did I owe and for how long?

I do recall my thirtieth birthday. It was in Lethbridge, Alberta in a hotel. Having co-facilitated a workshop, we were able to get to the tiny airport only to be told that the flight was cancelled due to a Canadian blizzard. The taxi had a difficult time returning us to the hotel. Hotels in Lethbridge in the seventies were not luxurious. My colleague had the flu and remained in the room for the duration of the evening. I treated myself to a banana split. The idea of turning thirty being a significant benchmark had eluded me. Psychologically it didn't seem like an issue. I was just glad to be alive. I would though have preferred dinner out.

My thirties were what I think of as stabilizing years. Allen came into my life. My knight in shining armor came with an old Lincoln, three children adult enough to no longer be living with him, and John, a First Nation's foster son, who would live with us. Recently divorced, Allen was no financial catch, and I violated my own vow to never again marry a man without money! Thank goodness I did. Four days into our marriage, he was in the Chilliwak cardiac intensive care unit. Heart! And for no reason you can fantasize! That was the beginning of years of health challenges.

Allen's quadruple bypasses of more than a quarter century were not occluded when the lymphoma struck. Following chemotherapy at 75, he began taking philosophy courses at the local university, scoring straight A's. When he wasn't working on his own book, he was practicing his cello. His resilience has provided us with many moments of gratitude, not the least of which was in 1996 when he had three cancer related surgeries in four days, was on life support for a week, only to have the cancer return in a year. More about Allen later.

Three weeks after our marriage, which took place when I was thirty-two, I began my life as a psychologist in a cancer hospital. At one level, I resisted going. At another, it felt like payback time. I knew I would go. I never regretted it. Being there was like entering into a foreign world every morning. I often thought on my way to work that somewhere in the city someone was doing his banking, someone was selling carpets, someone was being irritable with her spouse. It was hard to remember that every day ordinary things were happening outside of those walls.

In that building, life was concentrated. As part of the team that introduced psychological services for cancer patients into the public health system, I was about to be schooled in medical politics, the depth of the human condition, the injustices of fate, and the power of hope. For five years, I crafted a career amidst the gifts offered by those who suffer and those whose lives are dedicated to helping them. On occasion, it seemed like one or more of the "professionals" would lose sight of the intended mission. For the most part though they were a group of remarkable people doing an impossible job. As head of the service, I found I had a knack for inspiring, a talent for planning, and a hunger to understand the human condition. In the later half of my thirties, courted by the university, I recognized it was time to move on. Although not as personally gratifying as direct clinical work, the sphere of influence was greater through the channels of an academic position. As a way of saying goodbye, I wrote the book *It All Begins with Hope*.

I accepted an academic position and negotiated the rank of the Associate Professor. I had been explicit. I was happy where I was. If they wanted a rookie, they should hire a rookie. I wasn't interested in the position at the Assistant level. And I wasn't coming for an interview. They knew my work. The selection committee could decide on that basis and on the basis of my CV (curriculum vitae). And I wanted a window. I had been five years in an office without a window. I was appointed as an Associate Professor. They renovated an open space, and I got my window.

I recall my new department head stopping me one day and asking how I was enjoying my new position. Sensing my faint praise, he inquired further. I replied, "Nobody dies here. People are so involved with trivia. I guess that is the price of working with tragedy for years." I was startled at how upset people could get about a student turning in a paper late. For months, I went in on Saturday mornings like I did at the hospital, only to eventually realize there was no need to do so. Day after day, I was puzzled to find that I was often the last one to leave at five or five thirty. At the hospital, I was lucky to leave by six.

Clearly, there was much more flexibility in my new position. That was to be a blessing given a periodically ill spouse and an aging father, recently widowed. My mother died at of fifty-eight of complications from open-heart surgery. That left me the family matriarch and missing her terribly. She used to call every Saturday morning to remind me to take my vitamins. She was the one I called when I published a paper, won an award, or read a good book. She was the one who gave me wings to fly. I still ask, years after her death, when I am uncertain about something, "What would mom have done?" Only then do I know what I need to do.

A professor has to have a research focus. I found my research footing by doing a study of several hundred disabled teachers and publishing the results in a book entitled *Living with Broken Dreams*. In the process, I was introduced to the politics of research and research funding but also to the joy of working with a competent research team.

Teaching wasn't natural for me but I was good at it. For me, lecturing wasn't teaching. Teaching was engaging students in the process of thinking.

Teaching was finding ways to have students experience the phenomenon we were talking about. It was structuring learning to encourage integration of what they were learning with what the world would ask of them as practitioners. It was making them at least partially responsible for the learning environment. By the time I retired, I felt I had become a good professor. A wall full of accolades would attest to the recognition that came my way. Following my passion and matching it with effort was fulfilling. I was promoted to full professor in six years. That wouldn't happen these days. Nor would my hiring process! Applicants now face a rigorous process. I am not completely convinced that having candidates exhibited on the academic parade square ensures a more astute selection.

Decade five was about hope. Simple as that. Thanks to Allen and many dedicated people in the community, particularly Shirley Graham and Jack Chesney, The Hope Foundation of Alberta was launched. Initially the focus was on the role of hope in illness.

The early years of the foundation were iffy. No one really understood what we were trying to do. The corporate world supports what it understands – a cure for cancer, a chance for kids to go to camp, a place for handicapped people to get out into nature – but a center for hope?! Indeed, it was a hard sell and only the committed efforts of an incredible team accomplished and continues to accomplish an impossible task. Funding was a major challenge. Conventional research funding was out of the question at the beginning.

Day after day, I spoke to those without hope, those who had lost it and recovered it, or those afraid they might lose it in the face of adversity. Over time it was apparent that the sphere of influence would be much greater than the realm of health. Schools began to ask us to be involved. Professions lined up for experiences that deepened their hope. Over time we developed "hope focused practice".

Twenty years later the Foundation has become an internationally recognized center for the study and practice of hope, now known as Hope Studies Central (http://www.ualberta.ca/HOPE/). One can now take an undergraduate or graduate course in Hope at the University of Alberta.

A local college partnered with us to develop a Hope Studies series. Post-doctoral fellows and visiting professors have joined us in our efforts to understand hope and to apply it in our daily and professional lives. I wrote about hope, researched hope, stretched to understand what hope-focused practice would look like, met other hope scholars, and loved my work.

The end of the decade required that I practice hope in my own life when I had three abdominal surgeries in eight months, the same year that Allen had three surgeries in one week followed by a week in intensive care. The decade closed with us both in the recovery process. Anything else that happened in that decade is overshadowed by the focus on hope.

It was the decade of my professional highlights. I began the decade wondering if I was studying something on the fringe. I ended it with a sense of being on the leading edge.

As for my fifties, decade six, life seemed like a series of interruptions. I feel like I didn't get anything done on my own to do list or my bucket list. The highlights all seem to be lightning bolts during random storms.

Shortly after I had three abdominal surgeries in one year, Tom, my eldest brother, died suddenly at the age of fifty-five. Painful as it was to lose a brother, I ached to relieve the wound that grief left on my father.

Not long after, there was the car accident, compliments of a runaway utility trailer not correctly attached to an oncoming vehicle. It totaled our Taurus wagon and jackknifed into the windshield. That meant back surgery, shoulder surgery, TMJ treatments, treatments for a C2 injury in a special spinal care unit two hundred miles away, and other minor adjustments over a period of two years.

Then, Dad got ill. Cancer. Things didn't go well. He had a wonderful life and a difficult death. I wish he had mentioned I would be executrix of an estate that would have some challenging complications, emotionally as well as practically.

The weekend of Dad's memorial our twenty-five year old grandson collapsed in our rumpus room and underwent weeks of investigations that required that he and his mom reside with us for a period of time.

Concurrently, Allen was struggling with debilitating fatigue. The following year, he developed an evasive and serious condition that continued undiagnosed while it progressed. As part of the investigative process, Allen had an angiogram that seriously compromised his kidneys despite the good news that his twenty-five-year-old bypasses were in very good condition. He and the Grim Reaper made another deal and with a radical change in diet, he made a remarkable recovery.

In the meantime, our grandson was again living with us for five months as he stabilized his life. As Allen was recovering, I developed an unexplained case of cellulitis (streptococcus bacteria) that threatened my arm. Despite immediate attention and intravenous drugs, complications stole the better part of two months and thirty pounds.

As we emerged from that challenge, the phone rang on May 3rd, 2007. A male voice began by requesting clarification about with whom he was speaking. It was the phone call you never want to receive. It was the coroner. Our foster son, John, had died suddenly and unexpectedly. It took involvement with eleven organizations to ensure a full Cree ceremony. We hosted a memorial in the inner city several days later. It felt like we were hosting a farewell for John. His friends, grateful to gather, were obviously also grateful for his life. John was born with an optimism gene. His path was a difficult one but he charmed his way through each struggle. We had spoken only a week before. The lunch that we had arranged for the week he died was never to happen.

A month later, I underwent ear surgery to restore my hearing that had been further impaired by the recent infections. Having had an artificial eardrum since 1981, I was astounded to discover there was now a surgical procedure that could restore my hearing. My hearing was indeed restored but not without complications. Unfortunately I got a strep infection in the hospital. More antibiotics. Thank goodness Allen was continuing to do well.

Towards the end of June, another unwelcome call. A good friend had taken her own life only hours after we had had an e mail exchange. It left me with many questions unanswered to this day. In July, Molly, our faithful dog, who had had a progressive tumor on her hip had to be put down leaving a pawprint on our hearts that only dog owners would understand.

In the meantime, I saw my financial future eroded in the 2008 meltdown. At a whole other level, I cringed as our country seeped further into dispassionate policies like the sludge from our Oil sands seeping into our watershed, insidiously and toxic. Allen's long and difficult fight with advanced lymphoma followed only months later.[3]

However, even in this difficult decade, there were good things. A wonderful official retirement celebration. A kayaking trip in the Baja to prove to myself that I had recovered from my injuries. The rewards of a small private practice. A couple more books published. That brought the count up to nine. A grandson was married. Grand nephews were born. Friendships deepened. Thanks to air mile points there were several trips to Scandinavia. I reconnected with family I thought was lost to divorce. Getting introduced to meditation. Learning to be vegan (plus fish) and realizing that I liked it, not an easy admission for a meat eating farmer's daughter. Watching the Hope Foundation flourish. Seeing students of mine whose lives I have had the privilege of influencing, go on to be leaders in our field. Feeling my marriage deepen in so many ways. Getting off pain medications! Seeing my hair turn silver and not minding it. Not wanting to turn back the clock even though now, more is gone than is left. Wrapping up the decade with a nine-week trip across Canada in a camper van. Having the spare bedrooms remodeled into "writing studios" to host writers for those sought after time outs that are almost impossible for writers to take either because of schedules or costs. Buying and using that longed

---

3   Documented in *Zen and the Art of Illness*: Surrendering to the Moment by R. Jevne.

for Canon D30 camera. Doing the occasional project or presentation like the one hundred and eighty-three image digital slide show on *Photography as a Metaphor of Counselling*. Loved that one. It became the seed of a book now in process, *Photography for the Inner Me*: Everything you need to know you can learn from a camera.

After six full decades, it felt like it was time to reflect, time to ask myself questions about where have I been, what have I been doing, what I value, what I do, what I want, and perhaps what I need. It was time to notice what and whom I appreciate. It was time to take stock of the lessons, the ones I have learned and the ones awaiting yet more maturity; it was time to consider what I know to be true for me.

I am under no illusion that my truth needs to be privileged by anyone other than me, and I am wise enough not to take myself too seriously. Each reflection is inextricably connected to a growing sense of gratitude that lends itself to celebration and which, in this manuscript, is offered in the form of an essay.

Why a series of essays? "An essay is an impulsive meditation, not science reporting."[4] Now, if I just knew what that meant, I could be true to the genre. Nevertheless "an impulsive meditation" approximates my intent. Henri Nouwen suggests, "The deepest satisfaction of writing is precisely that

---

4   N. Taleb, p. xxvi.

it opens up new spaces within us of which we were not aware before we started to write."[5]

For the purpose of discipline, my own that is, I made an agreement with myself that the essays would be of a similar length, thereby limiting the number of tangents. The essays are not written *for* someone. Rather they are intended as clarification exercises, perspective-taking, vision-making, a thinking out loud reflection, a listening-to-myself project. Any value beyond the particular to the universal is purely accidental. There is no hidden agenda consciously lurking, hoping to be expressed. I am "writing to learn", not to instruct. I am writing to reflect upon, not particularly to describe, the narrative of my life.

As the writing continued, I encountered an unexpected pattern. At the beginning of each chapter, I spewed out confusing, even negative observations of the world I live in. Only when I skimmed off the froth of frustrations was the gratitude visible. Given this is a manuscript intended as celebration, there is a temptation to bypass or edit out the less than enchanting reflections on life. However, for me, dismissing the negative, would be denying part of the process that revealed the celebrations. By acknowledging the aspects of life that disturb me, I understand celebration to be a choice.

---

5   From Reflections on Theological Education by Henri Nouwen, as quoted by Phillip Yancey (2001) in *Soul Survivor: How My Faith Survived the Church*. New York: Doubleday.

Many wait for an additional decade or two before embarking on a conscious, extended reflection that captures the essential pathway of their life. This manuscript is meant, not so much to reveal where I have been, but to direct where I might venture based on experience and observation. I have no interest in consulting developmental psychology textbooks or attending life transition seminars for the newly or soon to retire. I simply want to think about my life and the place it has taken me – or me, it. A concern about being unable to clearly articulate my views admittedly haunted me as I began. There was an inherent trust that reflection would itself help deepen an attitude of life as a gift. It is a time of life when I think of setting my sail for the last storms in such a way that I might not whine on my way should the ship go down.

For Your Reflections

Celebrating Survival

If you woke up breathing, congratulations!
You have another chance.

Andrea Boydston

To be alive is the quintessential gift. Nothing is possible without breathing. That natural effort would cease without the marvel of my heart beating regularly in the astounding range of 100,000 times a day without my even noticing. Without that amazing automatic rhythm, I would stop doing that one essential task that ensures life.

Just as amazing as the number of functions our bodies carry on, mostly outside of our awareness, is the number of things that can interrupt our health, even end our lives. They are not as predictable as we might think. A mosquito can carry a deadly virus, yet we may walk away from a motor vehicle accident that twisted a metal vehicle frame like it was a candy wrapper. Sitting beside the wrong person on a long flight could mean exposure to life threatening illness. A bee sting could do you in under the wrong circumstances. Careless food preparation could ruin your week. A drunk driver can ruin your life. Sun lovers risk cancer. People continue to smoke, evidence that information alone doesn't bring behavior change. High risk and extreme sports are more popular than ever. Driving on Route 401 near Toronto should be added to the list of activities not allowed if you want life insurance, yet people continue to virtually ignore speed limits. It is a form of civil disobedience we seem prepared to tolerate despite some of the highest accident rates in the world.

We learn to brush our teeth and most of us

continue to do so on a regular basis. We supposedly learn the importance of healthy food, exercise, sufficient rest, and constructive relationships. We are bombarded with instant soups. We buy memberships to fitness centres we don't use. We work long hours, watch too much television, and divorce rates are in the range of fifty per cent.

Obesity is now an epidemic and anorexia is on the rise. Hidden additives and overdoses of pesticides and growth hormones sabotage healthy eating habits. Not everyone can afford organic produce or products. Years ago, one paid more for a food product with a preservative; now the higher priced item is the one raised without chemical pollutants. Fast food outlets regularly offer salads and continue to sell poutine and deep fried chicken. The conditions under which some animals are now raised and slaughtered is cruel, if not criminal. I can now purchase a week's supply of meals prepackaged. I just add water and heat them in a microwave. A generation of people is now unskilled at making so much as a homemade salad dressing, and waffles are something that you put in the toaster! Hospital food isn't much better. In many instances it is prepared off site. Asking for a vegetarian meal in a hospital is a health risk. Surely ill people deserve more than instant mashed potatoes, soggy green beans and a wilted tomato. Hospital food likely won't make you ill. Strep infections, now ramped in hospitals, will get you first.

Many of our health risks are self-induced by our culture and values. Buildings can have "bad" air. People go jogging on cement sidewalks among buildings that shut out the sun, weaving in and out of congested traffic while inhaling exhaust fumes. Our rivers are polluted with the residue of our "progress". We have overindulged to the point of harming, beyond repair, the very earth that nourishes us. We have made an industry of bottling water, and I fear the day we make air a commodity.

Our mental health is similarly assaulted. Our work world is now riddled with uncertainty. Work place abuse is common and often not subtle. Stress related conditions vie for top place beside heart conditions as the contenders for insurance benefits. The recent "boom" and "bust" has ensured that the average family cannot envision owning their own home, at least not without a forty-year mortgage. Financial strain is known to be a dominant contributor to relationship stress. If work doesn't stress you, the drive to and from work will. A one hour commute, considered excessive a decade ago, is now commonplace. Rare is the commuter who will not witness a motor vehicle accident each week. Clerical staff in most institutions has been reduced. When I lost the use of a secretary I shared with six others, my workday extended an hour a day. Email is itself a virus that has infected our lives. Texting has moved us one step further from face to face contact. We have road rage, and technology now keeps us constantly available to any one for anything. Suicide rates are not encouraging. In Canada, it is more likely if you are male between the age of twenty-three and eighty, that you will die at your own hand than be killed in a car accident. Many people cannot identify three people within fifty kilometers who can help in a crisis. Anti-depressant and anti-anxiety medication is being prescribed at exponential rates despite research that questions their effectiveness for many patients. Many health care providers are ill equipped to dispense hope. And often don't refer patients to those who address mental health issues. Unfortunately policy makers and administrators either don't know, or dismiss, research that confirms that attending to psychological needs can lower medical utilization rates.

Cutbacks in health care have increased care-giving demands of family. Downloading the challenges of caregiving onto the community in the name of "homecare" would be fine if there was a corresponding increase in resources to make the services viable. Although men are caregivers in some circumstances, it is disproportionately women who bear the brunt of providing or managing care for a family member in difficult circumstances. Statistics on the consequences of long-term caregiving are startling. The sacrifices required are often at an exorbitant human cost.

A recent jaunt into Canadian history reminds

me that survival has not always been an expectation. Whether a Maritime storm or a prairie blizzard, a rampant flu or a failed crop, early life in this country was demanding. Hunger and starvation were more common than we can imagine. Infection was almost a death warrant. Childbirth was inevitable and potentially life threatening. Illness or injury could mean the loss of the family farm and a life indentured to debt. There were no social nets, nothing beyond the charity a neighbor might extend.

So what is there to celebrate? So much! At a personal and a social level.

I have had childhood infections, serious chronic illness, eleven surgeries and periodic injuries that could have left me unable to do normal activities. My knee operation at seventeen is still holding. At thirty, I got an artificial eardrum. At fifty-eight they restored my hearing! Twenty-nine years ago a doctor sat on the edge of my bed in St. Mary's Hospital (Mayo Clinic) in Rochester Minnesota following a serious surgery that gave me a second exit to my stomach and said, "We hope we have given you a year."

I have had pneumonia more times than most people have had a cold. I have been visited by numerous "itises" – cellulitis, gastritis, pancreatitis, bronchitis, otitis (ear), and several of their cousins. There are still antibiotics that work for me. Logically, we use them as sparingly as possible. I have never doubted the integrity of any physician who treated me. Oh! One exception. He did, however, not count on being held accountable! He is dead now so we will let sleeping dogs lie. I have had health care professionals who missed the classes on patient communication, and I have had those who have been exemplars of compassion.

I appreciate the efforts of Tommy Douglas and his colleagues who brought a level of justice to the health domain of our lives. His selection by the people of Canada as the Greatest Canadian tells me that my views are shared by many. Medicare has meant that every Canadian is equal, or ought to be, in the eyes of a physician and the health care system. It means that being Canadian means sharing the risk that just living can bring. We collectively contribute to minimize the impact of tragedies or mishaps that would otherwise be translated into erased futures. Doing so without a profit motive makes ultimate sense. Even corporate driven governments admit profit-delivered medicine has no advantage to the patient nor to the cost of services despite considerable advantage to the shareholder.

As I visited with a young mother of four, a fellow patient in Mayo, I will never forget hearing her anguish as she described the cost to her family for her medical intervention. Her mature hope was to die quickly. Their house was already mortgaged to the maximum and surviving even briefly would mean complete financial ruin. She laughed heartily at the abandonment of so-called "insurance" that they had assumed would assist. Illness is expensive even with medical coverage. Ask anyone with a chronic condition. So I celebrate the people of this nation who brought in socialized medicine and those who continue to lobby on behalf of it. Those who think "I am not my brother's keeper" have likely never been the brother.

I celebrate the moms and dads, the brothers, sisters, grandmas, grandpas, aunts and uncles, neighbors, and friends who reach out daily to assist those who are temporarily or perhaps even permanently restricted because of health issues. They drive us to treatments, pick up groceries, send cards, bring over meals, mail letters for us, tell us stories, and kick our butts on occasion. The many not-for-profit self-help groups that advocate for those without a voice would be powerless without these thoughtful people. It matters not if they give an hour a month or are dedicated daily volunteers. Without them, the life of the invalid would be "in-valid".

I celebrate the number of times that fate seemingly intervened in my life. The right person at the right time was there. Luck was with me when having capsized my canoe in the Lake Louise rapids, I was unfortunate enough to have the rope knot itself around my ankle only to be rescued by two hikers in the area – one the President of a canoe club and the other, a first aid instructor. Just what the situation required! Years later in a rafting accident, I was rescued by someone who had just taken river rescue training in time to be available to me. I recognize times in my own life when I have been there unexpectedly for someone, like the fellow who had wandered all night lost in the foothills west of Calgary who stumbled out in front of my car. I had taken a wrong turn a mile or so back and ended up on a trail that was not intended for vehicle traffic. My error was his good fortune.

Like many, I have survived many mini-close calls with mortality. There was the time when I was travelling with friends west of Port Alberni. We stopped when we smelled gasoline to see if there was a leak in the Subaru van gas line or tank. Exiting the car, we followed the trail of gas until fifty meters from the vehicle, it exploded much like a 007 movie! Such is the lesson that there is a fine line between luck and destiny. Being on a plane that had an extended difficulty lowering its landing gear clarified that control is an illusion. Being a relative novice kayaker who survived 2 to 3 meter ocean swells in a storm, thanks to the instruction of a skilled guide, instilled respect for the value of being with the right people at the right time. Being part of a culture with generous access to media coverage of tragedy allows for comparisons that can only conclude that gratitude for my relatively safe life is warranted.

I celebrate what I can do for my own health. The knowledge base that helps me do so has been provided by researchers and practitioners, zealots and charlatans. It is sometimes no easy task to figure out the relative value of recommended health practices. One of my health rituals is writing. Journalling has been a constant in my life. The therapeutic effects are now clearly established by researchers.

Me meditate! I don't think so! Until recently. Still not regularly. Photography was previously as close to meditation as I came. However, meditation, now established as beneficial, brought a new celebration. Meditation brought a clear sense, a quiet sense, of how quickly my body and mind can restore perspective and energy. So I celebrate every person who has contributed to conventional and complementary approaches to health and well-being.

Appreciating survival is closely tied to celebrating my body. As the third child in thirty-six months, I may have started with a few depleted resources but none seriously so. My first hospitalization was at five weeks for ear infections. Raised on a farm, my body learned to risk. Horseback or sow-riding, it was all a thrill. I grew up with the wind in my face, the wheat fields taller than I was, and summer storms were a visual concert. Mud was not something yucky. The ditches were full of water in the spring, and rubber boots were often not tall enough to accommodate adventures. I never liked worms or spiders. My hands knew the earth from planting and weeding the garden alongside my mom.

My legs knew a long walk from herding cattle to the distant pasture with my dad. I loved the smell after a rain and was revolted at how a neighbor treated his dog. My body was the measure of experience. I lived in my body.

I celebrate the marvel of my own body. My fingers move across the keyboard without me telling each digit to strike each key. My feet know how to walk. My nose knows how to sneeze. My mind has the good sense to stop while I sleep despite perhaps providing insight or entertainment through dreaming. My stomach will repel anything it selects as being too demanding, and my bowels will dismiss the refuse and let me know in sufficient time that it is needing to do so. My facial muscles still smile, my "bad" shoulder can kayak again, and I can comfortably walk the recommended 10,000 steps a day. And look Ma! No canes.

I celebrate my body for responding to the many times it has needed assistance. We have a mutual appreciation of staying at a moderate weight. I also enjoy the sense of a feminine body, of surviving as female, not becoming without gender as I age. I love the curves and gentleness that are mine. Growing up a tomboy has left me with an adventuresome body, one that loves the texture of freshly cut hay, the tension of riding a horse newly broken, the thrill of shooting rapids.

I celebrate the simple awareness of my body. I

appreciate noticing it while not judging it. I am deeply appreciative of living in it. We have been friends for years, and I have never accused it of "failing" me. If anything, the reverse is true. I celebrate the ability to feel, to use all of my senses. As I age, I understand and accept my body will change; I cannot expect of it in my seventh decade what I could of my thirty-year-old body. In my case, it is almost the opposite. At thirty, my body was ravaged with illness. I am now quite flexible, strong, and decently capable of endurance. I can cycle forty kilometers and swim forty laps. My body is, however, still aging. Not long ago I asked myself "what do I know about my body?" The consultation led to this journal entry:

> I know the large joint on my right foot aches in the mornings. That the first four or five steps I take in my new day are seemingly re-teaching me to walk. The bottom of my feet feel flat and my Achilles tendon has to be coaxed into co-operating. I know I am cautious how I get in and out of the tub for my morning shower and that I wish we had foregone the oversized bubble jet tub for a double walk-in shower.

> I know I love to lull in bed in the morning. To prop up my pillows and read, difficult as it is with bifocals. The perfect morning follows a solid sleep, begins with the awareness that, although I have obligations, I often have no agenda driven by time. That I can mobilize according to my own

timing. That I can sip the hot lemon Allen has brought me as if it was the nectar of the Gods.

I know the face in the mirror is someone else's, a much older woman than I am. I push up the skin along my jowls to remind myself of who I am, the me I feel I am. My face is not the only place where gravity has claimed my youthfulness. My breasts have lost a little of their firm roundness. The cheeks of my buttocks, although firm, are no longer smooth. The scars of multiple surgeries, mostly abdominal, I wear as trophies of survival rather than as defects to be camouflaged by full briefs.

Silver is dominant in my hair now, and it is rather flattering. I have not acquired the brittleness, the dryness of post-menopausal hair. When I had a perm I recognized the look of the "older women" of my childhood who baked ginger bread men for us after school and who attended "Ladies Aid" every month. I have gone for a perky haircut, feminine but not permed!

On occasion when I abandon my vegan preferences, I still love a 10-ounce prime rib, without the Yorkshire pudding. I hate gravies and love my vegetables this side of medium cooked. I don't want my carrots the texture of banana. I still occasionally order the twelve ounce "baseball," medium rare, at The Keg. Mostly though, my body wants to nibble. Not cottage cheese and Melba toast. I can imagine a conveyor belt constantly at my side and me indulging in morsels every twenty minutes. A piece of buffalo sausage, cashews, left over rice noodles with tamari sauce and onions, a half an apple. It has never liked cheese. My low blood sugars are signals that I if I flood the system, I will stall. I now need a consistent fuel injection system. I know I still dislike breakfast, less so since it is likely to be soup or salad. The wisdom of my body is clear to me as I move more and more toward vegetarianism. It simply says 'yes' to what is healthy and sneers at indulgences that are nothing but invitations to feel sluggish.

My body still craves. Comfort food. Touch. Stimulation. Texture. Adventure. Mostly adventure. It longs for the energy, the capacity to fulfill the unlived dreams. I harbor the dream that I will one day kayak the Norwegian fjords or walk several hundred kilometers of Norway's Pilgrims' Way. It matters not whether I do it. Just having the dream is important. What came naturally for decades must now be intentionally recovered or guarded or strengthened. I welcome rest as a gentle friend, not as a necessary interruption of the day's activities.

I know my body misses things. Dancing until the band stops. Playing badminton aggressively. Even more, jostling for center court in a racquetball game. Riding horseback with only a hackamore. Eating two banana splits. Skiing full out without fear. Carrying an oversized pack into a secluded mountain valley. Feeling waist length hair flow over my shoulders on a Sunday ride on my 175cc Yamaha.

I know I am weaker yet stronger. I know if I carry two briefcases up a stairwell I can expect my shoulder and hip joints to scream by nightfall. If I sit too long those same hip joints feel attached to ligaments that are becoming beef jerky. I can, though, stand my ground in wholly new ways. The quality of my energy speaks of my solidness, of experience, sometimes perhaps even of wisdom. I run less, notice more. I put away things systematically as if the physical nature of my body extends to the physical domain of my living. I want consistent gracious control. Rushing has lost its pretend value.

I know the internal chatter has, for the most part, stopped. I no longer bombard my body with the demands of a multiplicity of voices, each with its own list of obligations. I trust my body to be quiet, to make choices, to knows its limits and to cooperate with planning in order to live within those limits.

I know the hurdles are getting higher. When I have a setback, I have to reach deeper into an emptying cavern for the will to overcome. At those times the pharmacy of remediation is enticing and more and more difficult to reject. The eyes of my physicians silently convey the hope that I will comply with conventional, often drug based intervention. I counter by announcing a long-range plan for an eleven-day dog sled adventure from sea to sea across northern Sweden. There is no harm in the dream.

I know I love the sense of claiming my body. The rhythm of a paddle dipping into the water under my power. The silence of a ten-mile bike ride, slipping past cattle whose heads raise momentarily, past farmyards hardly awake for morning milking, smiling at gophers caught between curiosity and fear. And endlessly and effortlessly moving under the Canadian prairie "Big Sky". Well, perhaps not effortlessly.

I know 'taking a walk' is still an effort at times. Not physically. It's that I resist routine. Plans to get in shape are easily dismantled and recreated. Always with good reason and good intention. I know, and simultaneously ill respect, the need to increasingly befriend my body. I know it wants a fuller commitment, a time of freedom from obligation, an opportunity to strengthen.

In the not so distant past, I watched Allen do whatever was within his control to pass through a keyhole to recovery from cancer. His hospital room was also my home for many nights. I could feel myself becoming sedentary. Since he was taking on a huge challenge, so would I. I chose to learn to swim. Someone was able to stay with him for the brief interval that it took me to begin the efforts. There was a pool near the hospital. There wasn't time for lessons. I watched good swimmers. I decided it couldn't be that hard and attempted to replicate their movements. My goal was to swim a kilometer on the day he had his last chemotherapy. And I did. Three days before his last treatment, I swam my first kilometer. On the actual last day of his treatment, three hundred miles away, the grandchildren, all competent swimmers, entered the pool at the same time, and we all swam an "honor" swim for Grandpa.

The physical exchanges over time are fair. I know graciousness without glamour. I know my physical being embodies my confidence; my presence, not my apparel will turn heads. My feet are not the only part of me that is grounded.

For Your Reflections

Celebrating Abundance

Abundance is obscure without gratitude.
Ronna Jevne

I sleep in a warm bed, bathe in fresh water, and clothe myself in apparel of my choice. Every meal can include foods that nourish my body, and I can eat virtually any time I choose. I need never be cold. I have ample warmth at my fingertips. I can reach for a thermostat or a sweater. Dry firewood is awaiting the fireplace should that be my choice.

My bed has color coordinated fresh linen, and my bedroom is free from vermin, the elements of weather, or the threat of abuse. On my bedside table are copies of the magazines *The Vegetarian, Photolife*, and *Shambala*. There are two books, *Into the Hurricane*, a documentation of the media and corporate efforts to misrepresent the intentions of the social democratic movement in Canada and a copy of an unread novel. Unquestionably, I have the resources to attend to a variety of interests.

Our well supplies fifteen gallons of fresh water per minute. I can thoughtlessly run the tap while brushing my teeth or bask in a warm shower daily if I want to. Soiled, even slightly soiled clothes, can be washed at a whim. Biodegradable detergent is my miniscule contribution to the ecology. Our front yard is wood chip so we don't use precious water to fluff our ego with a green lawn.

Grocery shopping is predominantly driven by nutritional choices. When shopping, I now first peruse the organic section if there is one. Fresh fruit and every in-season green vegetable, nothing bagged, a few canned goods with no added sugar or salt, no convenience foods. There is no second thought about hosting company and feeding our guests well, providing those little extras - majoul dates, fresh herbs, perhaps shrimp in the starter salad. Our fish comes from a vendor who contacts us on occasion. No farmed fish. The majority of time we make our own soy or almond milk. That way I avoid the sugar and preservatives of commercial products. I am well aware that others who are lactose or gluten intolerant as I am may not have the time or dollars to accommodate their special needs.

We have a juicer, an expensive juicer. I feel the need to disclose, it was a gift. Nevertheless, we have a juicer. By using it, I can enhance my daily vitamin intake. As well, it means I can avoid the sweeteners and additives of commercial juice. As someone with a condition that seriously inhibits absorption, this means I have access to health enhancement shared by few.

As for my wardrobe, I have options when I dress each day. Things can be color coordinated and accessorized. When something is clearly out of style, should I notice, I can add something more fashionable to my wardrobe. Never having been a clothes hound I am, among my colleagues, considered very moderate in my choices, a trait also noticed and appreciated by my spouse. I have reached the age where my first consideration is my feet. Any uncomfortable shoes are collecting dust or have been forwarded to more enthusiastic feet. There are classic navy, taupe and black dress oxfords and a summer equivalent of each in leather open-toe sandals. No pumps as we used to call them. There is no need for them. When I need to wear something "dressy" I choose a skirt long enough to preside over low shoes. I am not fond of shopping or fussing. I own more than one purse but it is a rare occasion that can get me to transfer the clutter of the logistics of life to another container.

Sweaters are my thing. Takes years for me to recycle one. For that matter, I am slow on disposing of used clothing of any sort. It is a gene, I think. Grandfather couldn't resist bringing home other peoples' discarded articles. Dad couldn't part with anything whether it be the family car or an outdated suit. I hold the position that anyone who can part with a piece of heirloom furniture has, as we say in my profession, an attachment disorder. I have learned to edit my bookcases, kitchen, knickknacks, and wardrobe so perhaps there has been a mutation. The collectables DNA is weakening with each generation.

I seldom have had a car payment for long. We've never purchased a new vehicle but never had to drive a clunker. There has always been money to maintain both the mechanical aspects and the body of the vehicle we drive. I do not have to fear that our vehicle will fail to take me to my destination. We trade at 100,000 plus kilometers. Despite gas prices,

I can basically afford to fill the tank to go anywhere I wish when I wish. Our vehicle though is not a gas-guzzler.

All of the abundance to which I have referred to this point is material – is the "things" part of abundance. Even as a youngster, I was never hungry, always clothed nicely (sometimes in my cousins' hand -me-downs), could bring a present to any birthday party, had thirty-five cents on Saturdays, twenty-five cents for the movie and ten cents for candy. I had a small allowance and money for the county fair every July. Our family took an occasional moderate holiday usually combined with a family reunion or wedding. While accumulating four degrees, I never acquired the accompanying debt that was common even in my day. During my early university days, when I left home on Sunday evenings to return to the city in my four hundred dollar Volkswagen, it would be filled with some version of a care package to ease the expense of schooling. A county bursary and two-part time jobs were the further debt avoidance strategies. It simply never occurred to me that borrowing was an option. That was something you did to buy a house.

Much of my life, I have lived on a budget. Yes, an old fashioned budget. As a married couple, we have lived on a budget. I think of us as being good stewards of our money. However, our needs have seldom exceeded our income. Planning helps. It is good not to want something that is out of financial reach.

Our home is now paid for at a time when our income is substantively reduced. Good planning. Our travel has often been attached to professional obligations. We have had no need for a drink before dinner or for five star hotels. There are those among our peers who have traveled far more and with more class and those among our friends who have traveled far less. I feel it has been a gift to see tidbits of other cultures, morsels of other ways of being. The yearning for travel is now waning as the effort to maneuver in airports has taken the fun out of it. Also, the energy required to relate in another language now seems in excess of what I want to generate. We do though have an abundance of memories from our jaunts. Our charitable donations are almost all on automatic withdrawal so they are not subject to variations in our spending patterns.

When is abundance indulgence?

The Conrad Blacks of whatever proportion have shown us that to have abundance is not necessarily to feel abundance. To have had more than the basics of life on a consistent basis is truly a gift. There is something fundamental in place when survival has never been threatened.

I have never known 'not enough'. There always been enough food, enough clothing, and enough opportunity. Perhaps enough is not the same as abundance. Enough by the standards of our culture is unquestionable abundance in the eyes of most of the world. Even within our own country the disparities are distressing.

In our culture, there is seemingly never "enough". Happiness is always just one more purchase away. One more toy or gadget. One more appliance. One more adjunct to personal hygiene. Goodness knows how many unused electric toothbrushes don the countertops of bathrooms across this nation. The gap between the haves and the have-nots widens and the trivia marketed to the former now has to be aimed at our egos. The majority of new inventions are, for the most part, unnecessary. They are electronic trinkets that will need batteries in a month and in all likelihood will cease to delight us by that time.

Abundance is somewhat a dilemma for me. At one level Allen and I have less than many would suspect. At another, I feel we have more than is fair. I practically lose my breath at the present cost of a home, the outright gluttony of real estate speculation, the thousands impoverished by the "boom" and the "bust". The media keeps us afraid to share what abundance we have. Our political culture keeps our attention on "lawbreakers" rather than on immoral social policy. It is indeed a privilege to live in a political democracy. I yearn to live in a social democracy where we all share a responsibility, not only to see that people survive, but that they have access to what makes them human.

At some point I must wrestle with how much is enough? How will we, as a culture, collectively pay for meeting the expectations of a materialistic culture? A culture that has upped the ante to unrealistic levels- a very modest house is now $350,000. No one of moderate means can afford a moderate house, let alone afford to live in one of our major cities. What kind of pressure is put on the economy to feed this cancer? When does the pursuit of abundance contribute to unhealthy psyches, unhealthy families, and unhealthy communities?

The deeper inner abundance of my life that nourishes my soul began with loving parents, a sense of community, and brothers who stuck up for me. I was never out there without knowing someone was on my side. Never hospitalized without a plethora of cards voicing well wishes. Never acknowledged without the audience of both parents. Born in Canada, I was already tagged for a life of potential. Being Canadian is not an assurance of stability or opportunity, just more so than most, including our neighbors to the south. Free from verbal, physical, and sexual abuse means the scars on my psyche were not imposed deliberately. There is an irony in the reality that abundance begins with the absence of something. It begins with freedom from fear of starvation, the elements of weather, or the tyranny of religious or political oppression.

Abundance means my belly is full, my soul has at least the option of peace, and my future is not thwarted. Someone will be there with an outstretched hand if I fall. As the list of deceased peers mounts, there is less truth to that with each death. Will the repeating financial crises change anything? Will the policy makers balance recovery with humanness? Will the social net I have contributed to all my life be there for me if I need it?

Canada, although not alone as nations go, shamefully has danced around her obligations to the world. The garbage of our abundance has spilled over into a world that is limited in its capacity to absorb the wastes of our indulgences. Our gluttony, not only for food but also for entertainment, speed, prestige and convenience is killing us and killing our global family. Soothing our conscience with charitable donations to causes we helped create is hardly sufficient reparations. When agencies dispersing food (e.g. wheat) to starving nations are compelled to buy commodities at market price from the donating country, rather than purchase many times more goods from the host country, we can't call that "sharing our abundance".

A remarkable number of Canadians volunteer. I celebrate every person who shares their time, opens their checkbook, and takes seriously the phrase "my brother's or sister's" keeper. Imagine what would happen to social agencies, minor sports and amateur arts if all of the volunteer capacity were withdrawn? Our generosity, of whatever nature, is an immeasurable abundance.

What are my obligations, if any, given I live in a world of abundance? The first is to recognize that I am indeed privileged. What accompanies privilege? Can I ever truly understand what it means to look at the faces of three preschool children and know I cannot adequately provide for them today, or tomorrow? Can I know the experience of dependency on a long-term basis? Can I know the anxiety of having that dependency threatened? Can I understand the reality of the extended aloneness of the elderly? Can I know the anxiety or despair of the abandoned mentally ill?

Perhaps my first step towards gratitude is simply to notice. To notice how relatively random the distribution of abundance is. There is no denying I could claim to have worked hard, to have been recognizably disciplined, and in that way, have been the creator of my own destiny. What I can't take credit for is being born in Canada to loving and responsible parents, being endowed with very adequate mental and physical capacities, and having access to resources that allowed my survival.

I am very aware of others who have worked equally hard exhibiting equally constructive choices and life has not been as kind in socially conventional ways. Further along the scale, I am also aware of people who seem to be have been born with a silver spoon in their mouth; people who have simply been in the "right place at the right time". At the other end of the scale are people who have acquired all the culturally approved trappings whose souls were lost in the process.

I know there are those who would say we do choose our parents and our life's dilemmas. I have a hard time believing that everyone within one hundred miles of Chernobyl was, at unconscious predestined way, looking for a growth experience, or the people who perished in Burma in the tsunami were anything but casualties of nature. For me, synchronicity is intriguing. Believing that every moment of my life is subject to some unconscious force that made me leave at 8:04 am instead of 8:00 am therefore avoiding a tragic accident goes beyond what my rationale mind embraces. To be sure, should I be wrong, I would be grateful for the last task that interrupted me. At a deeper level, I believe such thinking, at least for me, represents the North American pursuit of control. We want to think that we control more than we do.

We want to believe thirty-second sound clips that tell us we can have whatever we want. The attraction to the doctrine of mystical destinies is well marketed. Psychological and spiritual gurus, all too often remarkably good entrepreneurs short on anything except charisma, promise the believer that the universe is a mail order catalogue amenable to individual wishes. First, of course, buy the DVD. Purchase the book. Attend the seminar. You simply need to learn a new and easy skill, drink a good tasting elixir, use a special machine, or just send money.

Even scientifically sound approaches can be usurped to the charlatan. There is clear evidence of mindfulness practices enhancing mental and physical wellbeing. However, it's increasingly popular to "Be mindful". Mindfulness has become a commodity, the flavor of the month. Gurus of mindfulness are popping up like the wild pansies on our wood chip yard. Like so many options, the challenge is to discern the authentic offering of a wise person from the self-made urban monk who supports his or her corporate abbey with multiple workshops and marketable disks.

When I left work early on July 4, 2002, having congratulated myself for doing so, I didn't expect a man would have neglected to ensure his utility trailer was adequately secured to his van. When the trailer came off its hitch, torpedoing my car and jackknifing through the windshield, I didn't have a sense my destiny was being fulfilled. Just gratitude that my destiny included survival. My life could have ended, could have been more impaired than it was. In the ensuing months my attention turned to gratitude. I confess on occasion wishing the offending driver would have said, "I am sorry". I do credit him with the integrity to declare 100% responsibility for the accident at the scene. Perhaps in this litigious culture that is more than many are blessed with.

Oprah has popularized gratitude journals. The intentional reflecting on what I have versus what I do not have is an important piece of the emotional fitness puzzle. When I look beyond my little world, beyond the obvious, my gratitude deepens. I need only notice the multiple opportunities for gratitude in everyday life. I am grateful for airbags that saved my life. I am grateful for the parent who worked two jobs to help his son or daughter attend higher education where they acquired the knowledge base to develop air bags.

When I eat, I am grateful for the farmer who has been underpaid for decades and continues to supply my table with abundance. I am grateful for the hundreds of organizations whose mission is to enhance the life of the disenfranchised. For the politicians who are constant reminders that we get what we vote for, and that we are privileged to vote at all. For the journalists who attempt to bring to our attention issues we need to consider. For the lumberjack who cut the tree that led to my new floor. For the activist who fights to protect old growth forests from the corporate logger.

Someone has made the cups I drink from, the frames that hold my photographs, and the microchip that drives my computer. Someone produces the garbage bags I use to dispose of my left over abundance. Someone else works long hours to produce my windshield wipers. And yet another works evenings to serve me on a special night out. A baker rises early in the morning so I can enjoy fresh bread.

A trucker is away from his family for days at a time to bring me essentials and trivia. Many are grateful to have the work. There are those in our country who are denied the gift of employment.

Abundance is not always concrete. A recent trip impressed on us just that point. It is not surprising to me that Newfoundland has the lowest suicide rates in our nation. Travelling in Newfoundland, we needed to replace our vehicle's aging battery. We were able to purchase a battery but, given it was a long weekend, there was no option to have it installed. A local person in line behind us insisted that we follow him home where he and his young son proceeded to install the needed battery. His simple response was, "We can't be having you think we don't care."

On another occasion several days later, I found myself in the emergency room of a small town awaiting attention for an infected foot. Being staffed with only one physician, the injuries of three separate motor vehicle accidents were serious and, of course, took priority in terms of treatment. Someone from triage came out to the waiting room, and addressing our friend Carol said, "Now we can't be having these people think we don't care. Now you will be takin' your friend home for supper and we will call when it's coming close to the time when the doctor will be able to see her." And indeed, that is just what happened. When it was my turn to see the doctor, he was as calm and compassionate as if he had just come on shift.

Somehow Newfoundland has been able to generate and sustain an abundance of community and caring. These gestures of kindness are contagious. They warm the heart, and they fuel the motivation to replicate the good deed.

I want to notice my abundance, feel it, not fear its loss, and not constantly assess it in relation to others. At my memorial, may the abundance they refer to be my laughter, my sense of purpose, my strength of character, my integrity, and perhaps even my wisdom.

For Your Reflections

Celebrating Allen

There is no substitute for maturity
and playfulness in a partner.

Ronna Jevne

Initially, I intended that these essays would be excessively constructive. The intent of this specific essay was to celebrate marriage. This would not be the place for my less than positive perceptions to find voice. However, in trying to write this particular piece I found myself nodding off with my own uninspiring commentary. Usually words come easily. Not always, but usually. In this essay, I had more attempts at a start than a Dodge van with a low battery. I couldn't jump start it for the life of me.

Bothered by my lethargic style, I let the writing sit for a day. In response to asking myself the question, "What's going on?" I didn't like the answer. On one level, I had agreed these essays were for me, not for an audience. At another level, I was censoring, searching for the politically or socially correct language, dismissing anything that was even etched with negativity. There was a sense of not being honest about something.

I believe I have a "good" marriage. One of those marriages many people would love to have. The kind that other people refer to when they say, "They have a good marriage". Friends rarely say "Ronna" or "Allen" without reference to the other. We are "a couple". Everyone knows we are a couple. Even our physician asks about "the other" if on a rare occasion we see the doctor independently. So, why not celebrate marriage or "my" marriage? Or "our" marriage? A litany of thoughts poured out.

I am convinced that marriage isn't that healthy, for women in particular. This is more than opinion. There are facts to back it up.

Married men have the best mental health, married women, the least. Women are now experiencing many of the stress related physical conditions reserved for men. Despite working outside of the home, women still do the majority of the domestic duties and childrearing. Fully a third of young women are choosing not to have children. When I look around at young married professional women I see people who are trying to do it all, trying to have it all. Those who put their career on hold express, at best, ambivalence about the delay. They have varying degrees of help from the men they married. For the most part though, these young women are stretched. They are less likely to watch a hockey game, have a beer or golf. Yes, they quilt or work out or get their nails done once in a while. They are though far more stretched than if they were single.

There are fewer grandmothers down the street and often no sisters-in-law stepping up to the plate to take the kids for the weekend. Even if they remember how to cook, no one is helping them put meals in their freezers for those difficult days. No reasonably priced day care exists so they take on extra work to have the privilege of being employed. Their health is at risk. They drive hours in one direction on Thanksgiving to be with one family and hours in the opposite direction to be with the other family at Christmas. Their professional lives are run by deadlines and unrealistic expectations often imposed on them by male dominated organizations. If they choose not to be in the fast lane, they are not considered material for advancement. If they are highly successful, it is best not to highlight it at home.

Many of these statements could be equally true for men. It is however, easier for a man to do overtime than his wife, and society will give them different labels for doing so. He has a demanding job. She is a neglectful mom. Even if no one says it or means it, she will still feel it. If she is sick, the kids will still get fed. If he is ill, he can forego his regular tasks. Moms still do the majority of cutting up the kids' meat and planning the meals. I acknowledge there are cultural and gender changes underway.

For the men for whom my comments truly do not apply, know that you are in the minority and that we need your leadership. Yes, there are changes. Let's not overstate how much has changed though. Think about it? Who buys the birthday gifts? Who sends the sympathy cards? I know things are changing and I am pleased that they are.

Many women still thank their spouses for helping with the dishes as if they are doing something extra. For many women, marriage is still an agreement to a one-down position. He gets his hunting or golfing trip before she gets her weekend with friends. He's manly for doing so. She might get labeled assertive, selfish, or even a "bitch" or a "privileged princess" for 'doing her own thing'. As parents on both sides age, she will do the majority of care giving, if not directly, she will manage the care. If there is a difficult in-law, she will be expected to be civil and to invite that person to family social events but he would not expect to invite the same person for a Sunday golf game.

More women are managing their own money now but have less of it than their spouses. By Canadian standards women still make approximately seventy cents on the dollar relative to men. The glass ceiling in the professional world is still very real, and women are disproportionately represented in clerical and service jobs. In other words, women still do the majority of low-paying jobs. You can argue - but that's not about marriage! It is if you read studies that conclude that the power in a relationship is directly related to the capacity to generate income.

So where does this leave me when my intent is to celebrate? I am disturbed by my own observations. My views verge on gender stereotypes yet many of my observations are supported by research, the rest by experience. Marriage is akin to an agreement to attempt survival together, but as women, it sometimes implies offering our lifejackets to those who are drowning. My sensitivities are not so dulled that I believe my experience is truth. I am curious to know how these paragraphs would differ had a married man written this chapter. However, I am left with a commitment to marriage as an institution primarily because it is likely needed for the social structure of our culture.

Marriage seems more about tolerating snoring, sharing pot roast, tag-team parenting, and going to parent-teacher interviews together. It feels like a matrix of coordinating schedules, budgeting, and attending family functions on time. Marriage is more the garment than the body. It is what has to happen for two people to function under the same roof, meet responsibilities, be good citizens, and stay sane. It feels more about the struggles of co-habiting than the joy of making memories. So what is there to celebrate? What is there for me to celebrate?

We live, not for the days, but for the moments. So for me, I celebrate, one of those moments remembering our wedding service as Allen looked into my eyes while he recited his vows with a combination of innocence, maturity, and gentleness that I will never forget. In that moment and in many to come, I knew the experience of being cherished. It was August 1, 1981 just above the banks of the North Saskatchewan River. One couldn't have wished for a more beautiful wedding day. Even though the mosquitoes were uninvited, they were memorable.

I feel I can still celebrate each and every vow taken on that day:--

Our vows were as follows:

Our vows are based on what we uniquely know of ourselves and what we believe to be essentially human. They represent an awareness of the exciting risk we are undertaking and a willingness to give up unrealistic myths. In committing ourselves to them we are affirming the natural human rights and needs that are their foundation.

the right to be respected

the right to be trusted

the right to have inadequacies

the right to feel and to express feelings

the right to privacy

the right to be yourself

the right to change and grow

the need to be forgiven and

the need to be loved.

Recognizing these rights and needs as the foundation of a lifetime relationship each of us wishes to declare.

I will recognize and accept that you have a past. That you have deep feelings for parts of your life that preceded me.

I will maintain old friends and develop new. Although you may be my best friend, I will not expect you to be my only. I will provide time to be your friend and to develop shared friendships.

My body and my mind I will treat as gifts, to be shared by both of us, to be kept well and healthy,

I will appreciate your strengths and not ask you to "Be Like Me". I will cherish your uniqueness and encourage your growth.

I will strive to understand our differences, seeing them as gifts, not problems. I will request, not demand, change.

I will use my strengths in our relationship, our families and my work. I will explore my weaknesses and be open to change.

I will have a dream and not ask you to provide me with purpose. I will negotiate shared goals and support you in your dreams.

I will give our relationship overall priority and join you in a vigil to protect us from the clutter of life. I will negotiate times and commitments that may temporarily unbalance our lives.

I will, though difficult at times, express my thoughts and feelings, rational and irrational. I acknowledge the value of both. I will recognize you may have a private life of inner thought that you may not always share.

I will seek:

> meaning in difficulty,
> fun in the serious,
> delight in the unexpected,
> joy in the everyday.

Three days later, I stood by his bedside in the Chilliwack intensive cardiac care unit wondering whether I would be widowed before the anniversary of our first week, yet strangely grateful that we were formally married.

Later that fall our first neighbor introduced herself over the back fence by asking, "Is there something I should know about you folks?"

"Hi, Ah...Why?"

"Because there is always an ambulance
            outside of your condo."

"Well, we have been having a few challenges."

The health challenges have been like storms, sometimes pounding in like a hurricane, relentless but short-lived. At other times, it has been like an endless dreary rain without even periodic sunshine. The interludes of fair weather are gifts to both of us. We had major celebrations for our tenth and twentieth anniversaries. By our 25th, it was almost embarrassing. We simply couldn't expect our friends to gather once again believing this might again be our last celebratory event. We decided on an Alaska cruise, just the two of us. Allen's energy had slipped below the measurable level again, and a week of complete quiet was his upper limit. It wasn't a good year.

A year later he was walking daily, writing a book, traveling across Canada and looking forward to university in the fall, having decided he wanted to pursue yet another degree, this one in philosophy. For us, uncertainty has been a blessing. The debilitating nature of some unremitting conditions suffered by many have not escaped our notice. I celebrate Allen's survival. His tangible presence is worthy of celebration. His continuing well-being in the absence of occasional and sometimes less than good health, we also celebrate.

Years ago when Allen was first ill, we coined the expression, "Makin' memories". Understanding that life was for us somewhat more obviously tentative, we navigated our way between obligation and opportunity. In some ways, we stepped further into the river of life, more into the intensity rather than back from it. Foster kids. Demanding work. Political involvement. Yet we consciously planned time outs. Trips happened when they were possible, usually as an addendum to professional commitments. We were good stewards of our finances. We acutely felt the threat of the lack of earning power prematurely arriving, and indeed, it did. Our values though dictated that we share resources in support of specific causes. As the years pass, I wonder if our tear in the ocean of concern made any difference. Every three months we sat down, discussed six topics and made plans for the next three months – health, family, friends, finances, careers and our relationship. I still have that planning binder. The adage "love is not looking at each other.

It is looking together in the same direction" took on new meaning. I grew to love this man in ways I had not anticipated and for which words are not easily found.

Marrying Allen has been one of the better decisions of my life. It was important that we marry. Neither of us wished an extended common-law relationship. The public commitment seemed important. Yet, it is not marriage per se that I cherish, that I celebrate. I celebrate this man who convinced me, and believe me those words are chosen intentionally, that he could commit himself to my well-being, that I celebrate.

I celebrate the phenomena of love that has played itself out in our relationship. What a gift to awake each morning beside someone who smiles. What a gift to have someone who will laugh even in intensive care. What a gift to share a life with someone who cares about the things and people I care about, not just with lip service but with his presence and our resources. What a gift to feel proud to be by his side at any event, whether that be a community picnic or a dinner with a political figure. What a gift to know we have a difficult decision to make and to know that we will talk it through as we have talked through every decision until it has felt right for both of us. What a gift to have someone agree to meet for a quick lunch and not be upset that we both waited in different restaurants (before the days of cell phones). What a gift to be encouraged to pursue my love of photography. What a gift to be partnered with someone who has an optimism gene and truly believes that he will emerge from each and every ICU admission, and does.

I celebrate the mystery of his individuality. Every year I realize I continue to know Allen. This man who I have tea with regularly, who is grandpa to those who call me grandma, who I know votes for the same candidatethat I do, and who loves to go shopping with me. We both hang our clothes from light to dark, and he appreciates a level of tidiness that approximates mine. I can predict what he will order from a menu. He can predict I will try on three outfits and buy none. We know where to take over for each other in the telling of a story. There has always been a shared bank account, and we agree easily where we need to be each Christmas. Our tastes in music and reading are dissimilar but respectful. If we are lost, there is a high probability my directional instincts will be more accurate than his. I wouldn't think of handling the vehicle maintenance, and Allen is kitchen-challenged.

Yet, the mystery of living with another human being never ceases. I can never really know what he is feeling as a tear comes to the eye of this former police officer as he watches Little House on the Prairie. He adores his children and they him but I am excluded from the first hand knowledge of the events he describes as his shortcomings as a father.

I can care deeply and listen intently as he describes his parenting efforts with humor or dismay. His gift to me is that he willingly, or with small prompts, has learned to share his inner world. I celebrate that we cannot "know" what each other is feeling, cannot "know" each other's motivations, and therefore are invited to an endless exploration to know each other. I celebrate that we don't assume we "know" the other's thoughts or feelings. Every day I have an opportunity to understand more about him. We may have become like comfortable slippers but we don't know where those slippers are walking in any given day.

Wherever we go we are committed to going there with respect. Our relationship has always had a civil tone. Neither of us agree with the school of thought that the relationship has not been tested unless you fight. When our grandson was married, he and his bride assigned someone to collecting on video, brief pieces of advice from those who attended the celebrations. Asked for ours, we quickly agreed and replied, "Treat your spouse at least as respectfully as you would a stranger in your home." How many times in the ensuing years since we made that agreement have I, when I was irked, stopped myself and asked, "If this was a stranger and I was irked, how would I express myself?" Not communicating immediately has saved hours that would have been required for relationship repair over the years. We also do our best not to share information the other already has. Occasionally it happens. For example, when Allen backed into the only tree in a campsite, I would have been wiser not to say, "You backed into a tree!" I celebrate our capacity to recognize silence as support.

On a day like the day we inhaled the culture of Quebec City and as he intently entered into dialogue with the tour guide about the Seven Years War between the English and the French, I was in awe of his quiet curiosity. Following the tour, I knew more about Canadian history but also more of Allen's love of history. Repeatedly, I notice how he sees things in historical context when I may see only an old fort. Without Allen, I would have explored no history, understood very little of the world of science, and avoided ever golfing. On the other hand, he may have worn fortrel slacks long after they were outdated, overindulged in unhealthy food, avoided reading philosophy, and have not developed a reflective dimension.

The ways in which we are similar likely account for our compatibility. The ways in which we are different have been our growing space. It is from our differences that I have learned the most. *Discovery, McCleans, MacWorld, The Monitor* from the Canadian Center for Policy Alternatives, anthropological texts and philosophical readings occupy his bedside table while mine is piled high with mostly unread books varying from Buddhist texts, to Canadian novels, to social science commentary such as *The Black Swan*.

Over the years a complete disconnect could have easily occurred. I celebrate that it didn't. Despite often not understanding the complexity of what Allen is reading, I sincerely invest time in hoping to do so. In like manner, Allen being inclined towards *hard* science willingly has explored ideas about qualitative research. Each of us had enough depth in our own fields to avoid the need to compete. Each of us acknowledges a virtual encyclopedia in the person who sits across the table every day. Believing that I cannot ever fully know this person with whom I share my day-to-day existence gives me space in which to continue that discovery. By assuming that the Allen I married is not the Allen I live with today, I remain open to learning about his world, particularly his inner life. Being in relationship with him, I continually learn who I am.

There will be, of course, a day when one of us will die. No euphemisms. No platitudes. No soothing the pain with a mythology that includes meeting again in the hereafter. Should that happen, it would be a welcome surprise. Our talks have included who we hope to be in the absence of the other. Our preference is to make every effort not to be less in the absence of the other, but to be more because we were in each other's life. We celebrate the strength the memories will bring.

Recently we were invited to the wedding of

the daughter of friends. They are a wonderful young couple. It was one of those ceremonies where I came away feeling like "this couple is going to make it. They get it!" Our gift to them was two special teacups with a matching plate, the kind of thing a grandmother might give. With it went the following explanation:

<blockquote>

The Gift of Tea

Sitting together, talking about our lives

Our inner lives, not just the hustle and hassle
       of life

Has crafted the depth of our marriage.

When we had tea in the early years

We planned

And planned

And worked out busy lives

So there was time for us.

We figured out which of the kids

Most needed our help

Which causes to support and

When to visit aging parents.

We made decisions about money

Holidays and careers.

We made sure that schedules

Included time for us

Even if we had to tell white lies to the world.

</blockquote>

And even then we overcommitted ourselves.

And now on Monday mornings we have tea
And talk about the grandkids and
Which one of them most needs our help
And which causes to support
And how to stay healthy
And what friends to cultivate
Knowing friendships don't happen by chance.

So our gift to you is teacups
And a little plate for snacks –
Nanaimo bars are our favorite
Majoul dates work well.
Nothing too unhealthy.
But nothing really sensible.

And a formal cake plate
So you can have tea with others
And look like you do it with class all the time.
So you can talk to them about
What's important in their lives
And exchange views about
A healthy Canada
And how you will make a mark on the world
And how families are something else
But you wouldn't want it any other way
And what life is teaching you.
In decades to come

We hope you continue to celebrate
Your presence in each other's life.

It's all in the tea.
We hope you will sit together
Talk about your lives
Your inner lives, not just the hustle and hassle
          of life
And craft the depth of your marriage.

For Your Reflections

Celebrating Friendship

A friend is someone who understands your past,
believes in your future, and
accepts you just the way you are.

Author unknown

As a child I was the youngest of three children, the two older being boys. Living in a rural community the nearest girl was a mile away and, as I mentioned, she couldn't ride a horse. The next was five miles away, Catholic, and attended a different county school. There wasn't any going over to a friend's place to play. Tip and Lady were friends. Tip was part collie. Lady was a black mare, very child friendly. By age ten I was admitted to the boy's club and could shoot a pellet gun with the best of them. Skated pretty well too. Played ball as well as any of them. I was "one of them" and yet, I was on the outside. There was no sleeping in the tree house that I helped build. So who did I play with? Talk with? Tip. Lady. Until the day she died, my mom was both parent and friend. We didn't discuss personal issues – boys or disappointments or my future. We talked ideas and of practical things like what to plant in the garden.

In a rural community, friendship was inclusive. You didn't not invite someone. Birthday parties were community events. In those days, there was no hiring a magician and inviting selected students. Birthdays were for everyone: the boys, the few girls , the neighbors, my aunt Millie Everyone, young and old, came for birthday cake.

I reflect at times on what influence those childhood experiences had on my expectations and perceptions of friendship. Without play dates as they are referred to now, without someone to play tea with in the backyard, without other little friends from whom to infer what should or should not happen, I wonder if I am skewed in my understandings. My friends were my brothers, my mom, my dad, occasionally my cousins, the grown-ups who taught me to play crib. There was little sense of peer friendships. There was no talking about nothings allowed on the phone. We shared a telephone line with thirteen other residences.

Moving to the centralized school meant meeting new friends, something I had not had practice doing. Gratefully two friends, one in my class and one in the next class called on me at my first recess. I think they had been prompted by the teacher to welcome new students. We remained friends until high school when our classes took us other directions. Neither of them went on to advanced education. One took her own life as an adult.

In high school, I was on the periphery of another previously established group. Taken in, but not central to the group, I was just grateful to share noon hours with others. Being a student that had to take the bus, there was no opportunity for after school friendships. There were music lessons right after school once a week. The only school dance I ever attended was in a wheel chair after an illness in grade twelve. The seven of us continued contact for a number of years but geographical distance and life took its toll. Three of us still have close contact and a fourth connects whenever possible.

As I grew older, there was choir. I was an inept choir pianist. Every Wednesday night I did my best to accompany the local choir. Freeman, the director would give me two weeks notice if we were going to attempt a new piece. Following practice I was never left out of the coffee (hot chocolate for me) session that usually happened. When I say "not left out", it was not only that I was invited but someone would ask if our volleyball team was winning and how my studies were going. And would listen. I listened to the newest information on round bailers, and when I joined the women in the kitchen, I learned whose aging mother was having trouble remembering.

The women of the community cleaned chickens together, made lefse together, and raised money for the church by catering. There was never any question I belonged. In retrospect, I realize I was the only female teenager in the area. I wonder what the boys were doing? I remain endeared to those pioneer women who treated me as an equal, taught me how to slip the lungs out of a chicken with my forefinger and how to flip lefse without it tearing. Without them, I wouldn't have my love of entertaining or my sense of pride in the kitchen. They were friends, older friends. It was always a joy to get that uncensored hug from them even after I left home. They continued to support me with genuine pride in my professional achievements. Most are gone now but not from my heart. I had the honor of delivering the eulogy of one of the last of those pioneer women.

Friendships formed as an adult are different. There isn't the history. There are not the practical jokes, the failing math together, the winning tournaments together. Once in a while I meet someone I know I will appreciate over time; someone who hopefully will come to know me in a deeper way. New friendships come with built in limits. The level of disclosure and dialogue may be uninhibited but the expectation of what can happen given busy lives is best respected.

Friendship is one of those fluffy words that have such breadth of meaning that for me it lacks the depth of the very thing that it attempts to name. We have friends who... " so often means, "we have acquaintances who.." Where is the boundary? Or is there one? Are acquaintances friends in the wings? Sometimes I have found that "friends" I thought were in the wings showed up when friends I thought were front and center stage didn't.

There is nothing like the context of illness to clarify friendship. One morning Val, who I helped in an illness context thirty years ago, phoned to offer her help given our new illness context. Go figure. It was like those years had never passed between us. She offered an understanding that comes only from having also walked a path known only to the unlucky. Phone calls and e-mails from distant friends checked on us regularly. So comforting. Yet who could help get the groceries? Who might offer a moment to deliver a failed appliance to the repair shop? Who might spell off the caregiver for a needed few hours of respite?

So much of friendship is molded during difficult times. So much has to do with reciprocity. It's a delicate balance. Being willing to ask for help. Not imposing on others who have their own lives to live. In these days when families are hours or days away, friends become families-by-choice. I notice I am avoiding using names fearing I might leave out a helpful soul and inadvertently impose hurt.

Over one hundred "friends" came to celebrate Allen's 75th birthday on Boxing Day. More would have been invited but the venue was too small. Ten brought salads. Others helped cook the fourteen lasagnas and yet others prepared and served the ice cream cakes. It was a bouquet of friends from our many worlds, and Allen was radiant in their presence. We have had friends drop off the repaired computer, sit with me late at night in the twilight of a hospital room, send funny cards, and bake me gluten free cookies.

As I type, I realize "friends" do things. They come when invited, send regrets when they can't. They do what they can, and there is no hurt for what they cannot do. They may be quiet or loud, old or young, skilled or obtuse at seeing what would be appropriate. Intent is what matters. Whether I serve them home-made soup or a seven-course meal is irrelevant. What is important is that we laugh and talk about what matters. And we know that age will change us all, and we treasure the moments together.

Perhaps we have different friends for different purposes. Perhaps there are dining out friends. Play friends. Practical friends. Friends from work. Friends from church. I simply don't know. I take some solace in believing a friendship village can be a kaleidoscope. No friendship is cut from a cookie cutter. Each can be different. What I do know is that I am grateful for each and every person in my village on that continuum even if at times I am puzzled by his or her presence or absence.

I wonder how I measure up as a friend. How many times have I taken someone for granted? Have I received a gift or assistance and let the thank you I intended to slip off my to do list? How often have I failed to pick up the phone to say "hello"? How often have I let a birthday fade off the calendar without acknowledgement? How often have I failed to prepare a casserole or arrange a surprise? More times than I would like to think.

I have a pattern of being cautious of needy people, whatever that means. Am I afraid they will ask too much of me? Invade my physical or emotional space? Ask for hugs I don't want to give? Perhaps being in a "helping" profession, I have shied away from bringing my professional self into my personal arena. For the most part, I am an uncensored friend. By that ,I mean I feel at ease with people. If I find myself straining to be myself, or feel that my "self" is not welcome in the relationship, I likely don't call that relationship a "friendship". One of the markers of friendship is the absence of the need to tip toe around issues. Friends can agree to disagree.

I have friends who are politically in a very different camp in terms of what I think the world needs. I have friends who are deeply committed to religious views and doctrine that I find completely puzzling. I have friends who are so differently talented than I am that I wonder how we laugh together. I have friends who are so profound in their contributions to community I am humbled beside them. I have friends whose education and employment are completely outside of any realm of my own knowledge, let alone expertise. I have friends who are privileged with financial resources and physical health, and I have friends who are tormented with poverty and illness. I now have more female than male friends. Five of my best male friends have already died. The oldest was eighty-six, two of the youngest were fifty-eight. Although fewer now, my male friends are dear to my heart, welcomed and valued.

So, what is this thing I call friendship? What do I really know about friendship?

In the later years of my father's life, he buried many friends. Having lived in the same community for ninety years, there were few he didn't know and many he could with integrity call "friend". He once, in his simple wisdom, voiced, "It is one thing to make new friends. It is another to lose the ones you made the memories with".

It will not be long before I have accumulated fifty years of friendship with Irene. Fifty years without ever exchanging a harsh word. Having transitioned to retirement, she has built a home only minutes from me. That means time for tea and laughter and exchanging political views and whatever else "old" friends do.

I know that Irene is my friend. I know I can call anytime about anything. I know she will nudge me into laughter about my woes, cheer for me in my triumphs, help me in my time of true weakness. I am welcome, without invitation, at her table as is she at mine. I know because that's what friends do. Irene has taught me. That's what friends do.

I speak of her to others as "my sister-of-choice". She is the person that I trust with my fears; the person with whom there is no need to censor, no need to revise myself to be acceptable. She is the person with whom I can be irrational and silly and paranoid; the person who listens but holds back the advice; the person who says, "Do you have any cheesecake?" as a way of letting me know I have whined long enough. That's what friends do. They find subtle ways of telling you to get on with things.

I know our friendship may have been different if she had lived down the lane, if we had planted our gardens together, if we had shopped at the same local grocery - but that wasn't possible. Life took us to geographically separate places. We have lived our friendship for the most part in two different provinces. Had we been in closer proximity, perhaps we would have developed complacency. Perhaps our strengths in daily doses would have become irritants.

I know friendship doesn't just happen. We enter each other's lives consciously. We choose amidst demanding worlds to bracket a few hours here and there for a visit, to not lose touch. We understand that we stand on the periphery of each other's world; we understand that we are central to each other's day to day functioning, not by our physical presence, but by carrying each other in our hearts. That's what friends do. They make spaces in their lives, even in their busy lives. They don't demand more than can be offered, and they know it gets unbalanced sometimes.

We had to snatch time. Irene travelled a lot for her work. She has three children in nearby cities. She forfeits precious time with them to touch base with me. Taking an hour here, an hour there. I know if she says she is coming, she will come. I know if she says she is coming at four, she may be here at six, or even tomorrow morning, but she will come. I know that I am a small but important part of her life. I am mature enough to keep my expectations realistic. I know and admire that she *"people keeps"* other special friends. I know that I have no need to make her different. I love not being the same. Friends don't need to be exclusive or carbon copies.

Over time, the words of my eighty-five year old father take on increasing validity. Irene and I have been friends long enough that the memories have become legends that even her children can recite. The stories can be referred to with one or a few words. Simple mention of "the orange" will bring sufficient laughter to seduce a would-be audience to plead for the *rest of the story*. The "hunting lesson" story is another favorite fueled by an ever increasingly embellished description of Irene in a pink angora sweater on a cold October day wading through a slough well endowed with cow dung to retrieve a downed duck. It will bring delight to my soul to the day I die. If I die with a smile on my face, it is the reliving of that moment that has been recalled. That's what friends do. They help you make the memories.

We are seldom at each other's special moments. I have not seen her children graduate. She did not attend any of my four convocations. We make it to weddings, funerals, and crises. I was maid of honor at her second wedding. We basked in bridal privilege on that cold January 31, 1982, taking our time to get ready. Already twenty minutes late leaving for the church, we stepped out of our condominium to discover that the men had taken both cars. A desperate effort roused our next-door neighbor out of her bath, into her bathrobe and parka, and into her vehicle. It was too late to sing, "Get me to the church on time." We laughed the whole way. That's what friends do. They give us moments of laughter.

In 1997, when both Allen and I were desperately ill, Irene and Michael drove six hours to be with us for a few hours after we were both discharged from hospital. They made soup, baked muffins, did the laundry, and drove six hours home thirty-six hours later. They seldom even awakened us. They simply cared for us. We could offer only a faint thank you. That's what friends do. They take care of us when we can't take care of ourselves.

When Irene broke her pelvis and arm in a riding accident a month later, I flew to be with her when her daughters had to leave. I couldn't do much given my condition but my presence was witness to our friendship. Before I left I shared in the Cree sweat that was part of her healing.

Years ago when she had a post-operative complication, I flew from a conference to be at her bedside. My new Ph.D. was enough for me to announce confidently to the commissionaire, long after the front doors of the hospital were secured, that I was "Dr. Jevne" and that I was here for "a consult for a Mrs. Hannah on Station 30." I was dutifully escorted to her room. We spent the night together. That's what friends do. They appear when they are needed.

You would think that friends would remember each other's birthdays. Irene remembers mine. I notoriously forget hers. We exchange Christmas gifts, usually around Easter. We know that the designated gift giving times are secondary to the gifts of our presence. She was there for me years before as I awaited transfer to the Mayo Clinic for what was hoped would be life saving surgery. At five feet, seven inches and ninety pounds, no one was betting that my return ticket was a good investment. She was at my bedside until late the night before I left. That's what friends do. There are there in the dark moments.

Irene will do my eulogy. I can't know that she will. Fate twists our lives sometimes. But I know I want her to be the one who tells the stories, the one who says, "I know this woman and we are friends and I will carry her in my heart as she carries me in hers". I want the world to know Irene was my "sister-by-choice" and that this is my way of saying, "Wasn't I lucky to have a friend like Irene while I was here." She knows she is to put in the obituary that I want lots of flowers. I know she will dry them and mix them with my ashes so that I am never alone. She knows she is to put home made oatmeal cookies and red licorice in my casket. And she will. That's what friends do.

When mom died unexpectedly and prematurely, I was to deliver her eulogy. On the way to the service, I shared my doubt that I could do it. Irene offered to sit directly in front of the podium and, should I falter beyond recovery, she would rescue me. Allen, too, offered a way out if need be. They sat together. My two best friends. In the first moments of the eulogy, the grapefruit at the base of my throat seemed insurmountable. My eyes probed Irene's and Allen's for a brief moment seeking assurance of my options. A smile came across my heart. Tears were streaming down their faces. That's what friends do. They cry with you when your mom dies. I gave the eulogy.

I have idealized sisterhood most of my life. I love both my brothers dearly. There has not been a harsh word between us in our adult lives. I am not sure there was in our childhood or teenage years either but I can't swear by it. To have a sister was something that I thought was the answer to the longing for a playmate, a confidante, a consultant.

My mom called me "Sis" most of my life, and to some degree we had a relationship of sisterhood. She was the one I called if I had a paper published, purchased a new outfit, rare though that was, won an award or wanted advice on a workshop. Interestingly, I didn't consult her about the world of men in my life.

For years, I thought that women who had sisters had someone to shop with, someone to bring them chicken soup when they were sick, someone to be there in the audience at special events. I thought that without fail, they honored each other, supported each other and called to say hello even with busy schedules. I thought they remembered every birthday and cheered at every success. I longed for a sister. Longed for a place to know that I was welcome without invitation, a place where I was expected to help with family functions whether it be setting a table or creating table centerpieces, a place where I was a part of things.

I have wondered in this series of essays where I would talk about my other chosen sisters. I celebrate my sisters-of-choice as a special form of friendship. Irene is my oldest and deepest sister. There are others though that I feel I can call sister. Not all sisters are the same. Each has different strengths. In my case, all are geographically distant. In one case, across an ocean. Most are my vintage. However, following my mom's advice that it is good to have friends of all ages, I am aware of the friendship value and the sisterhood potential of several younger professional women who have included me in their lives.

There are two women who actually call me "sister", who made the bond conscious and verbal. I had known Sandi for twenty years. She and Rob were married the weekend after Allen and I were married which accounted for the fact that we were not at their wedding which was celebrated on my parents' farm. My mom was a stand-in mom for Sandi, mentoring her into the life of a farm wife that she was to be for at least a few years. Lynda, her twin, I met much later. Lynda was married to Conrad, a soldier in the Canadian Forces. On his retirement, it was her turn. The short version of her story is that she spent time in China learning the language and teaching English. Conrad returned to Canada, and although supportive, did not travel overseas again. Lynda returned home to be at his bedside as Pic's disease took its inevitable and fatal toll, quickly diminishing his physical and mental capacities. She has since entered into the adventure of a new marriage. One summer afternoon, some years ago, Sandi and Lynda informed me that they were coming for tea, and I would need to set aside a couple of hours. What unfolded was what one might call "a sister ceremony". Lynda conducted a Chinese tea ceremony in our gazebo. I was pronounced "sister". This was followed by what was for me completely foreign - the whimsical playing with capes provided for the ritualized experience.

Disappointed, I complied with their desire for no photographs. Their experience of being identical twins was one of constantly being photographed. My experience of photography was evidence that I actually existed. Only later did we understand each other's perspectives on photographing occasions. The relationship has deepened with our public commitment to be sisters and that part of me that longed for a sister has quieted.

For my sixtieth birthday, I took five additional sisters-of-choice for Thai supper, and we reminisced about thirty years of friendship. It occurred to me as I introduced them to each other, I was the connecting thread. They were not sisters to each other. They were my sisters. These are the women I will know until one of us dies. These are the women whose opinions I value, whose joys and losses I am willing to share. Most have birth sisters yet I am welcome in their world. These are the women I respect for what they have done with their lives. I am proud to call each of them "friend".

For Your Reflections

Celebrating Family

Call it a clan, call it a network, call it a tribe,
call it a family.

Whatever you call it,
whoever you are,
you need one.

Jane Howard

Of the reflective essays I am asking myself to write, this is clearly the most difficult. For many years, family has been both a major source of existential angst and my heart's desire. I have a family of origin, an immediate family, a stepfamily, an extended family, and what I would call a family of choice. Our efforts at a foster family met with humbling outcomes.

How broadly do I define family? As I have matured, I have opened myself to the fact that I am not separate from anyone else. Am I not sister to the woman who is at risk to be raped when she goes for water each day near an African village? Is the corporate tyrant who has made profit his God not in some way also my brother? Am I not daughter to the mother abandoned because of mental illness? Am I not cousin to the nurse who works shift so that my loved one may be comfortable? If I include all of humanity as family, what social obligations do I have? This reflection deals with family in a smaller context.

Being part of family

Without question, I was part of a family growing up, and I celebrate the gifts of those years, not the least of which is the storehouse of memories and the crafting of my character. I was the youngest and only girl in a family of three children. For part of the year, we were three consecutive ages. Being a girl in a rural community in which there were only two other girls within five miles meant I was often alone.

The boys were somewhat inclusive but logically I was on the periphery much of the time. I recall when I was in grade school envying the kids from the orphanage because they would have easy access to someone to play with. They would have undoubtedly been pleased to have my brothers and two parents who lived under the same roof.

I knew I was part of a family. Our family had meals together, attended church although not religiously, if I may pun. We ate at the table together twice a day. There was no conflict allowed at the table. And you ate your broccoli! Even my father who thought anything green but peas was probably meant for cattle ate his broccoli. We could eat in front of the television on Sunday nights in order to watch Walt Disney. The kitchen was mom's domain except for breakfast. Dad could make a mean breakfast of pancakes or eggs and bacon or oatmeal. Most mornings, there were orange wedges. He never resented mom having a sleep-in on one of the weekend mornings.

On many of the Sundays when we attended church, someone followed us home for potato salad, ham, and homemade buns. There might be a homemade pumpkin pie with whipped cream, real whipped cream. We said grace before most meals, mostly a rote version.

We shared domestic and outside chores. We had allowances, and we sold eggs to our teachers for extra spending money. We watched hockey night in Canada every Saturday night and Guy Lombardo almost as often. Everyone was expected to attend such rituals as anniversaries, birthdays, graduations and marriages. Funerals were on the "you're expected to attend list" unless you had a good reason for being excused.

Birthdays were always celebrated. I find it hard now when they are not. Every birthday was marked with a party and a cake. In my formative years, there was always a dime or two wrapped in wax paper embedded in the angel food birthday cake. We had our share of opportunities to attend summer camp, play a musical instrument, and, although vacations were brief given that we were a farm family, there were occasional holidays.

When I think about my city-raised mom, at nineteen, marrying the eligible bachelor more than a decade her senior and having three children in thirty months, I am struck by how different she was from the young men and women of today who continue to live at home into their late twenties. I love the words she delivered in one of her last speeches before her premature death.

I was not born and raised on a farm. I am the classic case of the country schoolteacher who married the eligible neighborhood bachelor. The year was 1945. I found the adjustments from urban to rural life almost overwhelming. I missed running water, especially hot – and inside toilets.

I was scared to death of pigs, cows, and even chickens. Thirty odd years later, and three children later, I am still afraid of cattle. I learned to drive a car, a truck and a tractor. I never learned to back up to an auger. I've experienced serious farm fires, the closing of the local hall, the centralization of the community school, and the near demise of the local church. I would never have made it without my sense of humor and that of my husband's. You need a sense of humor when the cat you thought was male has a batch of kittens on your new bedspread; your six-year-old gives your three-year- old a haircut; when your children have 4-H, confirmation class, ball practice, and music lessons all on the same evening; when you're trying to convince your husband that you really can chase the bull by hollering through the truck window.

What comes to mind when I think "family"? I think of a Norwegian grandfather who wanted us to speak his native tongue, who thought a good breakfast was sour cream on brown bread and who always had hard raspberry candies in the glove compartment. I think of a Norwegian grandmother who made the best fried potatoes I would ever taste. When mom was working full time, Grandma often did the family ironing. She loved to see us and often thought we stayed too long! That puzzled me for years.

Family times were always about food.

Christmas Eve meant lutefisk, boiled potatoes, melted butter and lefse, the traditional potato flatbread. Sometimes it included Swedish meatballs and marinated cucumbers. Dessert was English Christmas pudding with butterscotch sauce prepared by my English grandmother on those occasions when she joined us. Seemed normal, at least for our family. Both of my parents had only one living sibling, in both cases, sisters. Occasionally, we joined mom's only sister and her family in Calgary for Easter, Thanksgiving, or Christmas. Until we were young adults, we adhered to the traditions of my father's family.

I am appalled at how much I took for granted. I thought everyone had somewhere to be. Even into my twenties, I knew I would be somewhere with family for every scheduled occasion. I recall there often was someone present who otherwise would have been alone. It might be a recent widow, a foreign student, or a distant relative. I am embarrassed when I realize that until I began to host family events, it never occurred to me to offer a contribution to the meal.

Of my family of origin, there is now only my brother, Nels, and myself. I celebrate that we have become closer over the years. I was a complete enigma to him as a younger person. My mother died in 1984 at the age of fifty-eight. How I still miss her. How I still want to pick up the phone to report my latest purchase or achievement. My oldest brother, Tom, died in 2001 at the age of fifty-five. His unqualified acceptance of me gives him a place in my heart forever. My father passed away in 2005 at the age of ninety, having had a good life and difficult death. His unfailing commitment to the politics of the greatest good for the greatest number is imprinted on my social conscience like a hot brand. How he detested agricultural conglomerates he felt were unethical in their practices and greedy in their profit seeking.

Can I write about family with the credibility to adequately inform others about the nature of my "family"? As I age, it is a good feeling to be able to say that I celebrate the gifts that each person I call family has contributed to my development. At times, I confess to needing to explore what those gifts might be but the reflections have always yielded an awareness that they are indeed family, and I can learn from them. I do my best to celebrate their uniqueness and to honor the path that they are walking.

I am unsure if gratitude is synonymous with celebration, but it is sufficiently close to assist me in celebrating family. I am grateful that my family name came with respect and consequently with responsibility. Growing up a "Jevne" meant something, meant something in addition to growing up "Ronna". It meant you got respect in a store, you tried your hardest, you didn't cheat, and you took part in your community.

As a mature woman, I still mention that I am Tom's sister, or Nels' sister, or Morris and Jackie's daughter.

I know opportunists will think twice before overcharging me or providing minimal workmanship. No salesperson or tradesperson wants to risk being seen an untrustworthy by a Jevne. It isn't fear. It is knowing that their word carries weight. Being Kenny's second cousin means "don't mess with her".

When people say, "I knew your mom," their voice often slows, and there is a reverence in their tone. When people say, "I knew your dad," there is always respect in their voice. When people say, "I knew your brother," they almost always add, "You could always count on Tom", or some similar phrase. When people say, "I know your brother, Nels", there is always a genuine soft smile as if we both understand something for which there are no words. Clearly, Nels is a Jevne. You don't mess with him. He will never cheat you. He will help you if he can, and he will bring a smile to your face at the most unexpected moments.

There is something about being part of a collective that shares a name. A walk through the local small cemetery tells me that I am from a lineage that began here more than a hundred years ago. Tombstone after tombstone has a story I still recall.

Family is where we practice.

"Home is where no one ever forgets your name. Home is where no matter what you have done, you will be confronted, forgiven and accepted. Home is where there is always a place for you at the table and where you can be certain that what is on the table will be shared. To be part of home ... is to have access to life." [6]

I was the youngest and the girl. As a youngster I practiced holding my own against my two brothers. Maybe "against" is not the right word. There was never any unkindness on their behalf. I knew I had big brothers. When a grade three student threw his honey bucket lunch pail at me and cut my eyebrow, my brothers avenged me. Prior to one time when I was ill, all three of us had been constructing a sand box village. While I was unable to play outside, my brothers built roads and proudly graveled them with coal dust in the big sand pit as a surprise for me.

I practiced boy stuff with the help of my brothers. When I was well below the age limit for driving, Tom and Nels (also both well below the legal age) helped me practice driving. They set out stakes around the farmyard as a driving course. I drove the little International tractor. Back up. Go forward. Go between these two stakes. Back up between these and on it went. The finale was to put the tractor in third gear and give-er down the lane, without further instructions.

When I wanted to learn to hit the softball further, my brothers helped. They got out the hitting

7   Burnham, F.C. McCoy & M.D. Meeks . Love: The Foundation of Hope: The Theology of Jurgen Moltmann and Elisabeth Moltmann-Wendel. Harper & Row: San Francisco, p. 44.

stands from the local ball team and drilled me until every kid in the county knew when I came up to bat, to back up a sizable distance. Good thing they taught me to switch hit as well. It kept the outfielders guessing. Baseball was fun. Riding horses was even more fun. Dad would get me up at 5 a.m. to catch Lady, our child friendly quarter horse. She didn't want to be caught by an adult. Sometimes after catching her, Dad would let me cut the cattle he wanted from the herd. It felt great, much like the feeling of going to the stockyards on Tuesdays and hanging out with him while he bought hogs for the Livestock co-op. I was helping my dad!

When the boys got hockey sticks, my disappointed demeanor inspired Dad to turn around and drive the seven miles back to Wetaskiwin for a third stick. I was a better shot than both of my brothers with a pellet gun but was never invited on my uncle's annual duck hunt to Coronation. It gave me great joy to use my grandfather's double barrel twelve gauge and return home from a morning shoot by Coal Lake with more fowl than they would have after three days of huddling in a duck blind.

Mom saw to it that I practiced being a girl as well. My doll had handmade outfits. By the time I was in grade four I could not only set a table, I could prepare a basic meal. School lunches were my responsibility under mom's guiding eye. One year I won a red ribbon at the County Fair for the best school lunch. I also won the ribbon for the best date square and the best homemade salad dressing. It had butter and eggs yolks and real lemon in it. Between grades six and seven, I took a sewing course at the local Singer Sewing Shop. I took music lessons but only after I promised that I would not have to be prompted to practice. I kept my promise. Music was the beginning of developing the discipline that has served me well over the years. Homework was to be done after school, not when we were already weary and near bedtime. By high school, I had a pattern of sincere effort in school. My study habits made up for what I believed were moderate gifts of ability.

We all practiced respect, and we practiced responsibility. At times, there were four generations in the house. We were expected to never sass our grandparents - and we didn't. There was zero tolerance for any language that reflected ill-will or mean-spiritedness. Student council and 4-H were part of practicing leadership. Keeping a hen house of chickens and accounting for our meager allowance began the practice of fiscal responsibility. One didn't spend more than one had. Practicing waiting was part of understanding that no purchase was immediately mandatory. If it was a purchase that was truly important, it would be just as important tomorrow or next week.

Eventually I chose a life partner of my own and began the next phase of life assuming I would have my own family. Years later, I was able to smile when someone said, "Most of us had starter homes. And many of us have a starter marriage." I practiced - practiced trying to be what he wanted. Practiced trying to adapt to an ideal that was unattainable. Practiced trying to live on $328.00 a month and put him through university. Practiced trying to understand why caring wasn't enough, why budgeting wasn't enough, why no harsh words between us didn't mean our communication was healthy. Practiced trying to figure out how to be supportive to a moving target. Practiced delaying my own goals to accommodate his. I practiced silence. I practiced taking the consequences for my choices, practiced not being rescued, practiced requiring neither approval nor disapproval of my choices. I am sure my parents also practiced. Practiced standing by, knowing I was likely making choices that would make my life difficult. Eventually I practiced saying "Enough." Lesson learned.

Practicing also happens in the extended family. In mine, in ours, there are constant invitations to practice. I celebrate the lessons offered and even more so the lessons learned. The lessons offered by brothers, sisters-in-law, nieces, nephews, cousins, aunts, uncles and grandparents are part of forging who I have become, part of what and who I value, and part of what I understand as my own shortcomings.

Family is where we practice belonging. In many ways I have failed. Failed to negotiate a place in my family. Perhaps I have one. The challenge is to feel that place, to neither over nor under estimate it. Without children it is, I believe, more difficult to belong as the family of origin transitions to extended families. Geographical distance played its part. Being in a city several hundred miles away from either brother's family meant I was not part of my nieces' and nephews' lives as they were growing up. In retrospect, perhaps I could have been more intentional about being part of their lives. Birthday cards and infrequent visits are insufficient to build a relationship. At the time, it didn't seem possible to go to ballgames and graduations easily. I accept partial responsibility. I lacked the social confidence to invite myself to events that I might well have been welcome to attend.

Family is where we practice modifying expectations. What better place to practice accepting people where they are? Where else would I learn that small gestures count and large ones may be ignored? Where would I learn to deal with the disappointment of a forgotten thank you, which was so ingrained in my upbringing? During my childhood following every Christmas and birthday, there was a session at the kitchen table where we did the thank you card ritual. Where else but in family would I learn to forgive at a level deeper than required of acquaintances? Where would I experience the joy of giving the unexpected? Our families have been good families in which to practice. There is evidence in each of us of the gift of mutual lessons.

Families are where we practice negotiation. Where will we be for Christmas? When illness enters into life, it changes dynamics. We learn who will be there for us. Who will perceive our needs and reach out? Who will we be there for them when misfortune touches them? In day-to-day living we learn how well we will negotiate sharing our lives and resources in the midst of the tyranny of the work place, the inordinate demands of a frenetic life. The negotiation is not only about the practical, visible places of our lives. It is within us and with our partners. We learn what is reasonable to expect of ourselves and of others. The single detached person may yearn for inclusion but they do not have the struggle of balancing the expectation of two families during years when family is inviting, perhaps even expecting their presence. We yearn for fewer demands and yet, when they arrive, there is a vacuum we must negotiate with ourselves.

Family is where we practice sharing resources, where we decide to what degree to share resources. Time itself is a valuable commodity during mid-career. What are we prepared to share? What is expected that we share? How will we deal with the differences? What is the lesson that we want to convey to our family about sharing? What would they say about what we have shared? There is the issue of sharing with our larger family, our community, our little church, with the political party of our choice, with the non-profit groups that struggle in a society that is chronically reducing its public commitment to respond to suffering.

What is appropriate for family to know about what we are share with others? *Dr. Hudson's Secret Journal* by Lloyd C. Douglas had a profound effect on me when I read it at sixteen. I recently reread it and continue to concur with its philosophy of anonymity. Some of our gifts have been anonymous; some have not. Unquestionably though, our donations are a factor in the reality that I am still working part time in my sixties! I have no regrets for what we have shared.

Family is where we practice saying good-bye. Leaving home briefly is our first practice. In grade one, we leave for the day. We graduate to summer camp. We leave for the week. Then we leave to attend advanced education. Then we take up a life of our own. We learn to say good-bye even to life. Often, our first encounter with death is with the loss of a pet. I recall vividly the funeral we created for our budgie bird, an unexpected death. I don't know who wrapped our dead little bird in a coffin of tin foil. I do remember where we buried her. I remember with tenderness, a mother who let us honor our deceased chirper.

When it comes to people, as we age we learn to say goodbye to those who leave us. If death is introduced in a natural sequence, we say goodbye to grandparents, then parents, then friends and siblings. I learned my family was not going to talk about death. At least not to talk about that accident – the accident that killed Claude, the accident that, at ten, introduced me to death in a dramatic way. At fourteen, I participated in the dying process of Freeman, the choir director, a Jevne, a friend, a special person in my adolescent development. He willingly spoke of his regrets and good memories as I sat slipping ice cubes into his dehydrated mouth. He would leave us at forty-six, loved but with an unfinished life. It was during that time that the germ of interest in death and dying that dominated a good part of my career was sown.

As we age the line at the front gets shorter. I was with mom in the frenzy of rushing her back to the surgery that was unable to save her life. Allen and I were with Myrtle, Allen's mom – gentle, weary Myrtle - in the days and hours prior to her passing, as we were with my father several years later. Being there for my father and my mother at their deaths was a privilege. We were not able to say the words "goodbye" to our foster John, who after thirty years as our son died unexpectedly at forty-one. I take solace in a conversation that we had just a week prior and in knowing that we were always mom and dad. At one point I realized John would have to walk his own path. I could be upset or not. The choice was mine. The choice to love was mine too, and I am pleased he never doubted he was loved. In some ways, I practiced saying goodbye as a psychologist in a cancer hospital. Three hundred of my patients died. Many felt like family. What they shared with me made me part of their family. I saw families practice death and even more important, practice life, practice uncertainty. In the last decade, I have said goodbye to a brother, a father, a foster son, the family dog, a career, the illusion of security that accompanies youth, and to a sense of financial security.

Families by blood can estrange themselves but they are still family, and I am grateful we have none who have chosen that path in extremes. Families of choice present a different practice.

Sisters-by-choice have been my most wonderful practice. From them, I have learned consistency and trust and hope and courage. In some instances their families have become family-by-choice but not necessarily.

For me, family by choice has included our outreach to those who are without family. With family of choice I find it easier to be deliberate, to make it expressly clear that they are invited, that they are wanted, that they are cherished.

Families-of-choice may be temporary. They come into the fold as a function of being distant from their roots and as the Scandinavians say, "if there is room in the heart, there is room at the table". We are grateful for the many who have graced our table, who have left footprints on our hearts, and who continue to be part of our family.

We are grateful for those little ones who are now near adulthood and who still call us grandma and grandpa even though they know the bond is not based on blood. It pulls at the heart strings when it is time for them to move on to the next pieces of their lives.

Part of keeping a strong connection is acknowledging that parting is necessitated by life. We will hold each other in our hearts but the bond will be sustained with postcards and conversations on skype, not Sunday dinners.

For Your Reflections

Celebrating Achievement

What we achieve inwardly will change outer reality.
Otto Rank

It is not the mountain we conquer but ourselves.
Edmund Hillary

This is the essay that I hesitated to include. This is the   essay that bumps familial and cultural taboos about pride and speaking of one's accomplishments. Yet, in hundreds of private discussions I have had with ill and well people, the issue of "what have I accomplished?" comes to the foreground. We appear to have an innate need to accomplish, to have meaning related to how we use our lives.

Culturally, achievement is defined through male eyes. The achievements of women are often less valued. Traditionally we don't define relational or process outcomes as achievements. For me, there are two issues. First there is the hesitancy to voice achievements, and second, there is the exploring of achievements from more than one template.

Bragging was not an option at our family meal table. Good grades were rewarded though. Being first in grade 4 got me my first camera - a Brownie Starflash. I am hard pressed to think of any achievement other than grades that was reinforced in a concrete way. Rather, the fruits of my own talents or efforts were expected to yield their own rewards. There were red ribbons for track and field events. Collecting, cleaning and selling eggs yielded a small income. Practicing piano usually led to a better lesson, which meant stickers on my page. Practicing batting meant the opposing teams respected me when I stepped up to the batter's circle. Studying meant decent, if not excellent, grades. There was no bribing and no bragging. There was a caution not to place my brothers in the shadow of my achievements. At one point, I had to consciously assert to myself that it was okay to exceed the academic achievements of my brothers who were equally able but less inclined to study as they could anticipate futures that were not dependent on secondary education.

My father attended one year of college. The story goes that his father pulled him out of classes the following year to break land on the old Sablick place. He was meant for an intellectual life. In the one year of college he did attend, his association with Chester Ronning at Camrose Lutheran College, now Augustana Faculty of the University of Alberta, destined him to become a social democrat. According to the census, he was a farmer. A video of his life though would have revealed a ceaseless effort to encourage economic and social democracy. He died wondering if this country had regressed rather than progressed. The gap between rich and poor is greater than ever. It is not the dry prairie wind forcing farmers off their land but the corporate hurricane. A similar thing is happening to those who fish the seas.

He was a social man. He didn't know what discipline I was studying but he assured me if it involved people it would be rewarding. He sadly was never able to be at peace with his own choice about what to achieve. He was not a farmer at heart yet he couldn't sell the land. He couldn't be one of those farmers that used land as a commodity. He reinvested personal money in the farm while living out his senior years hesitant to spend money on small pleasures. After a bout of life threatening pneumonia at eighty-eight, he ventured into seeing more of what he felt he had missed. Through a series of West Jet airlines seat sale flights to Vancouver, he stayed with a friend and fulfilled a good deal of his new bucket list. He attended his first symphony. He learned to use the public transit, sat in on a court case, and visited a Buddhist temple. At home, he was a voracious reader. The phone would predictably ring before breakfast with a question like, "Did you know the population density of Brazil?" He inhaled a set of encyclopedias beginning at A and was constantly awed by how much there was to know. His Centennial Medal award has been misplaced. Likely my mom knew about it but it came to my awareness only because, as a young woman, I ran across it in a drawer of the dining room hutch. In his later years, I attended numerous celebrations and suppers at which he was honored for his lifetime commitment to the cooperative movement.

My mom was an equally remarkable and dedicated person. She mastered the art of being a full-fledged farming partner, no small feat for a city girl. Her concern for the toll farm living extracted expressed itself in her involvement in making rural life healthier. For her efforts, she is honored in the

Alberta Agricultural Hall of Fame. Later in life, she chose to return to university. At forty, she was already a grandmother.

What mom and dad accomplished was far beyond what is written on plaques and in newspaper articles. Both had what I believe all of us wish at the end of our lives - a sense of having done the best they could to live out the values they held, a family that stood by them and by each other, a circle of friends that was enduring and endearing. They both left this world a better place.

Mom was the person in my life who ensured there were little surprises in life. When I was little, she sewed. Sometimes we had matching outfits. There were always coins hidden in the angel food cake at birthday parties. At Easter, chocolate and marshmallow eggs always managed to find their way into the garden for an Easter egg hunt. Almost every September, there was a new lunch kit. Saturdays were library days and many evenings closed with a story.

Mom was a teacher that was educated in a post war teacher training program. I recall the year I was in her grade five classroom. The students with excellent handwriting assisted those who had more difficulty. Social studies projects were always in groups, and when we chose teams for sports, it wasn't always the best players who got to be captain, and players were not always chosen in the competitive way.

That same year, I was asked by a shy student who I didn't play with very often, why I wasn't her friend. In all innocence, I replied, "I didn't know you wanted me as a friend." I was actually quite shy and tended to be confident only on the ball diamond or in the gymnasium. She didn't play ball. When I said that I would be her friend, she asked me days later if I would come to her birthday party. I gave an immediate "yes". Knowing she lived in relative poverty with her four siblings and her widowed father. My mom made sure there was a special cake, and it was a great party. I remember thinking as I walked down that country road with four or five other little girls, "She likes me and I don't even have to play ball." The next year her family moved.

Mom ensured that I earned the first place standing that I achieved that year. She didn't risk anyone thinking that I had been favored. In addition though, I was learning that not all achievements are tangible. Clearly, for me, my values were being crafted in my childhood. I was learning, not only how to achieve, but what is important to achieve.

I am grateful for the many times she reinforced me for who I was, not only for what I accomplished. When I was dreadfully ill in grade 12, there was no additional pressure to complete high school that year although I did. She was the one who put her foot down about high school graduation. Both my brother and I were graduating the same year. The trendy thing was to go "to the lake" about twenty-five miles west of Wetaskiwin for a party following the ceremony. Those were in the days before "dry grads" were popular. Instead our parents, along with parents of other graduating students, hosted a barn dance for over a hundred grads. I recall my mom's concern as the organ from the local music store was being lifted using hay slings into the barn loft.

When I was dreadfully ill in my late twenties, she was at my bedside. She was the one who called the Minister of Transport in Ottawa to get a flight out of Edmonton when there were none to be had because the Commonwealth Games were on. That flight to the Mayo Clinic saved my life.

Mom was the problem solver. The creative one. There wasn't a problem that didn't have a potential solution. One of her common expressions was, "If it is impossible, it will take a little longer." When she passed away suddenly at 58, Dad did his best to take over. He asked me to teach him to cook, and eventually he could host a decent dinner party and make a wicked chicken soup. He never missed a birthday. In all honesty, there were years when I didn't have the heart to say I might like to do something other than to be with my dad on my birthday. In retrospect, I am glad I never did. And, there was always a gift that I know he personally wrapped. Missing one index finger, he never mastered the art of tying a bow.

How does this relate to my sense of wanting to

celebrate achievement? I certainly want to celebrate the achievements of my parents, whether that be my dad's contribution to the first Rural Electrical Coop or my mom's contribution to the mental health of farm women. They were mentors of achievement. They lived the words I often heard my father say, "Things don't just happen. People make them happen."

Parents are instrumental in conveying to their children how things happen. In grade five, a conversation with mom changed my life. There was concern expressed on behalf of the physical education teacher that my breathlessness from running bases was serious enough to consider limiting my involvement. In those years, I had what would now be called exercise-induced asthma. Mom was a teacher in the same school. I remember the place where we had the conversation. I remember what I was wearing. I recall the feeling she was going to say "no more ball". Instead she said, "if you are going to play ball, you are going to have to hit the ball further". With the help of my brothers and their little league equipment, rudimentary as it was, I did indeed do just that. It became a metaphor for surmounting challenges.

In another instance, I remember being startled when I was in grade eight, and my teacher said disparaging things about a student in the classroom in the student's presence that would diminish the self-esteem of even the most confident young person. Disturbed and puzzled, I informed my mom, who at that time, was a teacher in the same school. I believed she would do something about the discrimination. Her response remains vivid to me even to this day. It propelled me developmentally into a next stage. Her steady, quiet response was, "What are you intending to do about that?" Wow. It had never occurred to me that I would be the one doing something. So, I did something! I ran for student president and asked the targeted student to be a running mate as candidate for secretary. We won. And the remarks stopped.

Mom's unique ability to be in the background at the right time was truly a gift to my maturing adolescence. Somewhere in the process, I also learned from both parents that everyone achieves according to the opportunity, support, or talent available to them and that because I was well endowed with each, I had an increased responsibility to apply them for communal benefit.

Before going on with this essay, I have been to the fridge three times, thrown a load of washing in the dryer, considered vacuuming, taken a walk, and answered two phone calls that could have waited. I think the issue is a resistance to publicly itemizing what I believe constitute my achievements. How am going to do this without falling victim to the voice in my head that associates describing success as absorbed self-interest? I am going to approach it as an experiment. I can concern myself with feelings later. What have I achieved? Just list. No judgments.

No editing.

- I learned to ride horseback early.
- I never sassed my grandparents.
- I almost always did my homework.
- I played ball well. I did most sports well.
- I got my Grade IV Western Board piano despite having virtually no talent.
- I scored over 95% in all four years of music theory, once getting 100%.
- I learned to drive a tractor by the time I was ten.
- I could shoot an adult gun before I should have been allowed to have one.
- I never got sent to the principal's office.
- I was student president in Junior High School.
- I got my driver's license on the first try in a near blizzard.
- I passed grade 12 despite being absent for three months due to illness.
- I won a scholarship to a summer program at the University of Saskatchewan when I was fourteen. Because of my age they had to get special permission to allow me to attend.
- I won lots of events at many track meets.
- I finished university without debt.
- I learned to kayak despite being a non-swimmer.
- I earned three graduate degrees.
- I survived several life threatening conditions.
- I never, at least to my memory, have had a harsh word with either of my brothers.

- I maintain a clean and orderly home.
- I make a great vegan muffin and an awesome tofu cheesecake.
- I lay a beautiful table for special dinners.
- I was promoted to full professorship in six years.
- I wrote and published a number of books, book chapters, and professional articles.
- I managed to see a good chunk of the world on moderate means.
- I speak rudimentary Norwegian.

I would be remiss if I didn't acknowledge my sense of accomplishment in establishing group counseling services in the "Talk Shop" of the 1700 student high school where I first began my counseling career. I look back with satisfaction at the part I played in establishing psychological services at the Cross Cancer Hospital in the days when psychosocial oncology was non-existent. This was at a time when physicians were at the top of the food chain in the health care world and were not about to consider the potential contribution of people equally but differently trained. Among my greatest satisfactions are the stories I silently honor that reflect the difference in individual lives because I was there for someone in a way that they needed. Perhaps I was even the voice that they had lost in the presence of family or health care providers. Several of us across Canada began CAPO (Canadian Association for Psychosocial

Oncology), and there is now even an international psychosocial oncology organization.

The Hope Foundation of Alberta was crafted by so many but initially co-founded with Jack Chesney, Shirley Graham, and myself and in all fairness, with my husband Allen who is not on the plaques. He has though has been honored by the Foundation as a "Hope Ambassador" and by the province for his ceaseless contributions to it over the years. To see it more two decades later, morph into an international leader in the understanding and application of the phenomena of hope is indeed a confirmation of the relentless initial efforts it took. To have achieved the level of cooperative effort and supportive working environment that still exists, is a legacy. I love that organization. It isn't easy to raise funds for something that is intangible as hope and yet hope is so necessary to the progress of understanding the human spirit and harnessing it.

Hmmm. The experiment of writing out my achievements wasn't that painful. It is not about the volume of achievements. I have resolved that life is not a competition. The issue is the right to say what I have accomplished. Perhaps by doing so more women will refrain from minimizing what they perceive as accomplishments in the arenas in which they play out their lives.

There is a degree of satisfaction when I reflect on the accolades. They number fewer than many, more than some. None are in the big league of acknowledgements. They represent only public acknowledgement. Many have worked as hard with equally valid visions, and public recognition has not come their way. Among the accolades that I am fond of are the Queen's Golden Jubilee Medal, Global television's "Woman of Vision", the Dick Pettifor Award for "Outstanding Contribution to Psychology in Alberta", and the YWCA "Woman of Distinction for the Social Sciences".

     If you look at my vitae, the more than eighty pages of accomplishments are a very dry read. They don't represent the wonderful people I met on the journey or the growth in my intellectual or personal development. Nor do they represent the achievements of those who went before me, those on whose ideas I placed one more brick. I struggle with the idea of "intellectual property". To the best of my ability, I acknowledge the contributions of those who have gifted me with their thoughts. I verge on despondent when I read the work of others, professionals or students who do not acknowledge their forerunners. I shake my head, someplace between discouraged and angry, when I see my own words blatantly usurped in another's text. And it happens.

     In the bigger scheme of things, what does it mean to achieve anything? I am a grain of sand washed upon by an ocean of anonymity. In the greater scheme of things, whatever others or I might think of as an achievement is but a footnote in an obscure book. I acknowledge how insignificant I am. In less than a decade or two, I will be a name on a gravestone, and my name will be fading even for my family.

The essence of achievement is personal. Who I am, who each of us are becoming, is also an achievement. Although far from the person I hope to be when I leave this world, I have an inner life that is essentially peaceful. The storms pass rather quickly and are addressed deliberately. I assume no immunity to distress. I hope only to achieve an increasing ability to place the events of life in perspective, to take responsibility for my inner life despite the chaos of our present world. I have hope that at times I mirror my quiet into the chaos rather than mirror the external chaos in my soul.

The concept of achievement is to a large degree cultural. In our culture, it is comparative. We learn in subtle ways from early on that our worth is comparative. As I take stock of my perceived achievements, I consider also my attitude to the achievement of others. Can I look at each and every person with curiosity and make a sincere effort to understand what he or she has achieved? Can I look beyond the "products" of their lives and into the processes of their lives? Can I accept that being a good citizen, an honorable person, a constructive parent, or a consistent friend are the achievements needed more than ever in our community, in our nation? Can I enjoy a homemade soup in a humble home with the same respect as a five-course dinner in an elegant home? What do I respect as achievement?

I recognize that far too often we assume a strong relationship between the observable achievements and one's work ethic when that relationship is not necessarily there, in either direction. Someone may have worked hard with few observable results while others have simply been in the right place at the right time. I have yet to achieve the capacity of complete non-judgment about how others spend their time and resources. I do though, respect that there is often a rest of the story that, if understood, might enhance my tolerance – or deepen my intolerance.

It is hard for me to accept those who take the path of least resistance. Those who choose to smoke despite the evidence of harm. Those who are couch potatoes virtually addicted to the television. Those who have never had the joy of going the extra mile. Those who chose never to reflect, who seemingly have no inner life. Who never ask themselves how much they could be. Those who seem disinterested in what there is to learn, who there is to meet, or what there is to contribute. For me, these people are different than those who might have fought the good fight and lost, or never had a chance at any normalcy and turned to substances to self-medicate the pain. I have more respect for a thief who steals for his family than a con artist who is good at computer fraud or a CEO who swaggers up to the trough of corporate profits.

I will continue to feel a success if I can continue to find the good in those who puzzle me and not lose hope for change in that which appalls me. I believe it is an achievement, at least for me, to wish no one ill-will, yet not lose my voice about those issues that I feel harm us all.

I celebrate the achievements for which the rest of the world has personally recognized me. There is, though, a whole other dimension to achievement. When all is said and done, time in the limelight is but a paragraph of the entire life story. It is the story of the outer life. The inner life is the one that sustains me. For many years I asked myself periodically, "What is the next step in my development as a professional and as a person?" The latter is now by far the stronger focus.

I am reasonably confident that I can claim the journey so far has included being a cherished wife, a valued friend, a respected colleague, a well-intentioned citizen, an appreciated step mom, and a loved grandmother. As I age, my choice for further inner growth remains best said in the words of the poster that used to hang in my office during my stint as a high school counselor, "May I grow firmer, warmer, simpler, quieter."

I have on occasion been given feedback that I

am very goal oriented. Were I to have the opportunity to do life differently what, if anything, would I add or delete? There would, I think, be no deletions. There are two domains of my life that I might address somewhat differently.

I would be more aware of how to prepare financially for retirement. I do not resent a single dollar that we have contributed to causes so am I not sure if we could have done anything differently. I might have done it with greater awareness of the consequences.

The other dimension that I would have paid more attention to would be my physical fitness. The passion for professional challenge often meant that I was using timethat I might well have invested in remaining physically active. Most nights I wasn't home until after six, and my days started early. Many weekend hours went to professional tasks. With Allen ill and alone during the day for parts of our life, I was unwilling to increase his alone time by going to a fitness center in the evening. With that said, given my health history, I am in remarkable health. I sometimes describe myself as a vintage car - great quality but needing regular attention. Recently, I accomplished my goal of cycling forty kilometers and swimming forty laps.

We did what many would think of as an abundance of entertaining. In some ways, it was an accomplishment to have lived as balanced a life as we did, given two people with passionate professional lives and inclined to believe that we could make a difference, albeit in very different ways. Hosting was our privilege and our "village" was the enduring outcome.

What achievements do I look forward to? What do I feel is important enough to use my life towards its achievement? Again there are two dimensions: what the world will see and what I will know. Both are represented in the vision statement I wrote for myself several years ago:

- to use my creativity, wisdom and sense of adventure towards a meaningful life expressed through relationships, photography and writing;
- to deepen my spirit, strengthen my family and enrich my community and;
- to make visible the complexity of the human experience.

I am at that age where I am bluntly aware of my failures and cognizant that many of them are not reparable. I first noticed them as repeating themes in my journal - a shortage of time for myself, financial anxiety heightened by the 2008 financial crash, and lack of community. In other words, less personal time than I would like, less financial security than I would like, and less access to like-minded persons than I would like. I am at that age when I recognize that my whining isn't necessarily reality based. As a therapist I know that the source of our emotional pain is often not well correlated with the reality of our lives. Feelings are feelings. Reality is something else.

Four good friends joined me on a Zen and the Art of Photography course. The freezer is filled with options for unexpected company. A similar situation exists with regard to our finances. Although I don't have a pension, we have been good stewards of our money, balancing expenditures with experiences, and I still have income generating capacity. As for time, it is a sparse commodity in our culture. There are few obligations imposed by anything outside of my personal choice and situation.

The issue of community for many years was the wrenching shortfall for me. We cannot expect our small families to be communities in the way families historically once were. Distance and the demands of our culture mitigate against it. Community is often forged from work settings; for others, it is through connections of their children. For yet others, it happens through fraternities of faith or politics.

For most of my career, I listened to the woes of people whose stories I cannot share. The therapist/ client relationship is sacred, not unlike that of the priest/parishioner. Confidentiality is sacrosanct. In addition, psychologists are ethically obliged not to have social relationships with clients and former clients for extended times. Consider that the majority of my clientele were terminally ill clients and it is not surprisingly that work was not a source of enduring social contact. Those brief encounters of weeks or at most months with clients, were though formative to my maturity, each and every one, a gift. When I closed out my files at the hospital, just over three hundred of my patients had died. I had not forgotten a single face. The community of amazing professional caregivers were an incredible team who worked selflessly to accomplish an impossible task. We were, though, less likely to socialize than any group with whom I ever worked. Many of us were workaholics. Having a professional life of 24/7 was a choice. No one holds a gun to our heads to do those extra hours. For the most part, those hours were freely given in the cause of making a difference. I think though we had all had enough of death at work. We didn't gravitate towards those with whom we shared vicarious trauma. Despite that, four lifetime friendships were born of that era.

I failed to have the foresight to cultivate community except one by one. I am under the umbrella of no collective. By involvement in life and death issues so consistently, my tolerance for an afternoon of beer and superficial chit chat is under developed. I am at the age where the likelihood of cultivating a sense of community is low. It is not probable, but perhaps it is still possible.

I am grateful to Susan Pinker who wrote *The Village Effect*. With her insight I was able to notice that although I don't have "community", as in a social contact originating from a shared bond, I have a wonderful village of unique, caring, talented friends. I celebrate my village.

I am at the age where I am willing to voice the painful realities that emerge from the awareness of roads not taken in the hopes that others who reflect with occasional ambivalence, will wince less at perceived mistakes and embrace them as part of the journey. I have no need to ruminate about the paths not taken. I am grateful for the lessons, grateful for the companions, grateful for the landscapes I have visited. I celebrate the future that holds itself open to new paths. I celebrate being at the age I am; the age where I feel good about who I am.

For Your Reflections

Celebrating Spirituality

The most beautiful experience we can have
is the mysterious.

Albert Enstein

May the God whose name I do not know,
guide my day.

Ronna Jevne

Spirituaity is the buzzword of the new millennium. Religion is out. Spirituality is in. Gurus are popping up everywhere. For an adequate exposure to the self-appointed priests of our culture you need only browse the nearest bookstore. Be prepared if you wish to be fully initiated to attend weekend retreats and listen to hours of follow-up DVDs purchased through the internet on Pay Pal. Usually they are anti-dogma, although most have not taken so much as an undergraduate theology course. The real challenge is sorting out the authentic spiritual mentors from the well-intentioned charlatans escorting you along the spiritual path of least resistance. In many instances expect that nothing is required of you. You will simply be provided with an abundance of resources if you are "open" to the goodness of the universe that is awaiting your next workshop registration and product purchase. Many of the movements have characteristics consistent with cults. Perhaps, the flood of today's marketed spirituality is a sign that people are searching for answers. That in itself constitutes a reason for celebration. The flavor-of the-day spirituality, however, should be required to pass a minimal test of rationality.

There is a rise in mega churches that offer both community and anonymity, provide everything from Sunday School to basketball, have multi-media church services, a counseling ministry to help you recover from anything, and a volunteer honor roll for acknowledgement of the dedicated. In some instances, no social contact with the outside world is required. You can study, sing, deal with abuse, and enroll your children in summer camp all in the same building. A country club could offer less. However, believing in God and often a specific version of God may be the membership fee. Often, questioning is discouraged.

Approximately seventy percent of Canadians and ninety percent of Americans indicate that they believe in God. Those whose belief in spirituality use the word "God" less often than those with declared religious beliefs. The word "God" carries the weight of centuries of unfortunate associations. In a world more and more dominated by science, the word "God" implies a Santa who watches over us and depending on whether we are naughty or nice, determines our eternal future rewards. Usually God is a "He" and comes with a user manual for each denomination or religion. He, and he is almost always HE, is a source of unconditional love except for the ten rules, which if broken, can send us to perpetual suffering in a place called hell. Puzzling fellow. Yet, many know a gentle, compassionate, consistent non-gendered God, an endless source of strength. Present day theologians span the continuum from literalists impelling us to accept "God's every word" to those with such liberal views that theology is hardly recognizable from philosophy.

I remain puzzled that the most religiously

right States in America publicly execute more inmates than all the others put together. I am further confused when I realize that the same people who want to legislate women to have unwanted children tend to vote for capital punishment when society fails those children long enough that they end up in the penal system. I share the concern of Robert Masters in *Spiritual Bypassing*. He defines spiritual bypassing as "the use of spiritual beliefs [and practices] to avoid dealing with painful feelings, unresolved wounds and developmental needs".[7] He warns against spiritual beliefs becoming "metaphysical valium", "spiritual bibs", and cautions against becoming a "harmony junkie". As one friend so bluntly described her own explorations, "I am searching for a spirituality that is not based in stupidity".

If life is a pilgrimage, perhaps the destination is a mature spirituality. As a pilgrim, I enjoy my journey. I claim to only enjoy the search.

I look at the phenomena of spirituality rather simplistically. I believe spirituality begins with a search for meaning and purpose.

I make no assumption about the origin of the urge towards the spiritual. Some simply, without reflection, adopt the spiritual tradition of their childhood without serious consideration of

7   Masters, R. (2010). *Spiritual Bypassing: When Spirituality Disconnects Us from What Matters*. Berkely, California: North Atlantic Books. p. 1.

alternatives. Trusting their heritage circumvents the search.

Whether beliefs are inherited, whether there is a benevolence (altruism) gene as is now proposed, or whether individuals feel that God is personally addressing them, few would reject the human need for meaning and purpose. The experience of community then reinforces a code of conduct that often is derived or interpreted from the source of the prescribed truths. Whether the spirituality is embedded in religious doctrine, examined or not, or grounded in the age old need for meaning, for me, its expression must meet the criteria of practical wisdom. What does it look like when I live it? Secular or sacred, God or no God, surely the spiritual dimension of our lives implies an inherent ethic of respect and justice.

Philosophizing about spirituality perhaps avoids addressing the direction question of, "At a personal level, what do I know about God? What do I know in my heart of hearts - not what did I learn in Sunday school? Not what am I supposed to believe."

I actually hesitate to say anything about God. I equally resist dismissing the idea of God. The adamant position of the raging atheist seems as uninviting as the dogma of the fanatic. When it comes right down to it, the only honest answer is that I simply do not know anything about God. Ask me to write about the sacred or the spiritual and I might be able to call on my tacit knowledge, the knowledge somehow embodied from my experience. Ask me about God and I get tangled in semantics and in cultural skirmishes about religion and morality. Having a graduate degree in Theological Studies has not ended the questioning. Rather, it introduced a comfort with the questions.

I know that my roots are in Christianity, and that it is hard to dismiss the God of my upbringing, the one my grandmother consulted for the latest list of sins. The one in whose name she berated me for attending mass with a Catholic friend. Her god is a male, three-in-one god, immaculately-conceived-by-a-woman.

I cringe at public events when someone still says grace that begins with "Our Heavenly Father" and ends with "In the name of Jesus we pray". Not because it is wrong. Rather, I ache for words that include us all. In the context of tragedy, or as a defense for war on anyone's behalf, my hair curls and my nostrils flare when I hear patronizing things said in the name of God. Can God ever be a convenient excuse to harm or to fail to see harm?

The God of Convenience seems silly to me. The one who is on call for my trivial requests as if the universe is a lunch menu. The one some folks thank for a parking spot when they are in a hurry. The one who functions in lieu of Santa Claus and who knows if I have been good and doles out rewards in proportion. The one who is supposed to be on my side in a court case or in a war.

I know I am reluctant to speak openly of experiences others might describe as God. I am unsure why. Perhaps because the word God is simply a word, a word that means something different to different people – a word that simply does not capture my experience of the sacred. Perhaps the sacred shall always be private and personal for me. I abhor the place in the Christian worship service where parishioners are to turn to those nearby and offer a handshake along with the words, "Peace be with you".

The culture of worship is a constant barrier for me. There is perhaps a biting sting to the awareness that the person who anonymously shakes my hand on Sunday may feel no inclination or obligation on Monday to provide a casserole if I break my leg. Then again, the millions of daily acts of kindness are evidence that many will do just that.

There is little accommodation in the standard worship service of the psychological preferences of those of us who are, by nature, introverted. I have wondered if I might find comfort in a Quaker service where there is no requirement to recite, socialize or sing.

I still love the familiarity of the old hymns, lighting a candle in an ancient cathedral, and the solitude of being in a sanctuary alone. I know there are times when a quiet voice speaks to me from an unknown depth. I know I have glimpses that life and death make sense. I know there is an "Other" in me.

I know when people are sincerely gathered in the name of God something happens. I recall as a teenager, the experience of the oneness as five thousand of us kneeled together for communion. The feeling was similar to the humility and deep quiet I experience in the rituals of the Soto Zen tradition.

I know there is a rhythm to the strength of my knowing. At times, the intimacy seems undeniable. At other times, the distance seems insurmountable. I catch glimpses, sometimes longer than other times, of the sense of being at home, the unquestionable truth of a presence that is not essentially me. The presence is essentially "other" than me, yet is me. I know it is more than the power of love, more than the beauty of nature, more than the strength of relationships. The glimpses are there. In the mystery. In the depth of my marriage. In the warmth of the autumn breeze. In the capacity of a parent to sacrifice for a child. In the brush of an artist and the bow of a cellist. In the commitment of a life long friendship. In the soul of the opponent to an injustice. For me, the mystery is sufficient. Graduate education in theology deepened my sense that "God is at eye level" rather than embedded in a doctrine.

Raised by parents committed to social democracy, not surprisingly the "social gospel" has become part of my worldview. The essence of the message is that this life is not only about us; it is about being part of a larger community. We are not entitled to bully others, use more than our share of resources, exclude others on the basis of religion, color or creed, or flaunt our privileges or our talents. I didn't think of that as spirituality or as religion embedded into daily life. It was more like the responsibility expected of being a good citizen of the world. It is more the logical outcome of decent character development.

Books like *The Little Book of Atheist Spirituality* and *Religion for Atheists* point out that spirituality is not interchangeable with belief in a deity. For me, it is more about living from the heart, training the heart to enter into "obedience to the moment". It is about noticing the richness of what is in my awareness at any given moment. It is about noticing that I have choices in those moments.

When coffee is spilled on my Berber rug, I must choose whether the rug is more important than the dignity of the person who caused the mishap. Spilled milk, in this case, spilled coffee, is important. It builds character. It makes us notice what we value.

I take issue with anyone who says they "know" what happens after death. I accept that they may hold strong beliefs about such. I am, however, no longer drawn to debates with adherents of the "truth", including those who are adamant about the errors of religion. Atheism to me is no less a doctrine. A deep reverence for the mystery of life seems to be where I land. It leaves me with ample room to celebrate spirit.

How do I celebrate my spirituality? Every spiritual tradition to my awareness has a catalogue of rituals and ceremonies to mark the significance of times and events that symbolize their beliefs - the First Nations' sweat, the Buddhist retreat, the Christian communion, and the Jewish Bar Mitzvah, to name only a few. The ritual of pilgrimage crosses many faith traditions.

How, though, do I celebrate? What do I celebrate? Raised in a Lutheran community, I adopted, without reflection, the belief system of my forefathers and mothers that was transplanted from Scandinavia. They brought with them a tradition of community and a clear set of do's and don'ts for life. My folks were supportive of the role of the church. Religion though was never a central topic of discussion at the supper table. We simply learned our verses and took part in the expected.

However, after an out of body experience following an illness in my mid-teens, the need or pull to attend conventional services mysteriously simply faded. It not only faded, it simply passed. There was simply no longer a need to recite a protocol of prayers or to have a set of prescribed beliefs.

I do continue to have favorite scriptures from the Christian tradition.

The first is:
Corinthians 13:4-7 [8]

> Love is patient, love is kind. It does not envy, it does not boast, it is not proud. It does not dishonor others, it is not self-seeking, it is not easily angered, it keeps no record of wrongs. Love does not delight in evil but rejoices with the truth. It always protects, always trusts, always hopes, always perseveres.

The second is*:*
Ecclesiastes 3:1-8 [9]

> For everything there is a season, and a time for every activity under the heavens:
> - a time to be born, and a time to die;
> - a time to plant, and a time to uproot;
> - a time to kill, and a time to heal;
> - a time to tear down, and a time to build;
> - a time to weep, and a time to laugh;
> - a time to mourn, and a time to dance;
> - a time to scatter stones, and a time to gather them;
> - a time to embrace, and a time to refrain from embracing;
> - a time to search, and a time to give up;

[8]   Corinthians 13: 4-7. *New International Version (NIV)*
[9]   Ecclesiastes 3: 1-8, *NIV*

- a time to keep, and a time to throw away;
- a time to tear, and a time to mend;
- a time to be silent, and a time to speak;
- a time to love, and a time to hate;
- a time for war, and a time for peace.

This second passage is a beautiful piece of literature that places me in time and is congruent with the influence of the Zen tradition to which I have been drawn later in life. Its focus on questions about how to best live this life appeals to me more than the conjecture that I am pleasing a deity.

I celebrate the sheer existence of spirit. What an amazing phenomenon. Nothing implies sadness so much as a statement, "she is like a zombie." To be without spirit is to somehow miss the essence of being human. A zombie doesn't laugh or cry, doesn't hurt or offer compassion, lives with apparent lack of passion or disappointment. To have spirit is to have the breath of life within us.

I have, for as long as I have memory, understood that I have an inner life – a spirit life, as distinct as my physical life. As a child, when I would dream, I would inquire of my mother in the morning, which world was real? As a young person, I felt moved by ritual, touched by the mystery of life, intrigued by the uniqueness of different species, awed by the beauty of the sun breaking through fog.

"Spirituality is the practice of spirit."[10] I accept it is my responsibility to care for my spirit. It is my responsibility to ensure that I listen to what it needs, that I nurture it, exercise it, rest it, invite it to deepen and grow. My spirit yearns at times for adventure, at other times for solitude. I yearn for community, at times for aloneness. My spirit has loved kayaking in a storm in the Sea of Cortez, snowshoeing in a dense forest, hosting a formal dinner, meditating in the silence of a zendo, writing long into the night, sitting with a dying elder. When something is right for my spirit, it is as if time stops. I surrender to the moment. There is an honoring of being where I am.

I celebrate the people who, for me, seem mentors of what it means to be spiritual. Spiritual people are for the most part recognizable. Whether the spiritual mentors are high profile or as invisible to the general public as my recently deceased 98-year-old great aunt Elise, a woman of wonderful joy and enduring faith, these people seem to have heard a call. And they are "more" for having listened.

The high profile ones including such people as Nelson Mandala, Mother Teresa, Mahatma Gandhi, Martin Luther King, and Jean Vanier are all driven by a compassionate call to better the lives of those they can see at eye level. The Dali Lama's presence is, I am told, quieting to the spirit. Thomas Merton felt deeply the call to a monastic life. Many of us recognize the

10   Kovel, J. (1991). *History and Spirit: An Inquiry into the Philosophy of Liberation*. Boston: Beacon Press, p.198.

deep sense of integrity that accompanies a spiritual person. They live what Matthew Fox would refer to as a "spirituality of compassion" which he suggests is "the fullest experience of God that is humanly possible." [11] For Fox "compassion is not an ethical system". Rather it is "treating all creation as holy and as divine".[12] His words feel right in my heart, right for my spirit even though I might use different language.

Unlike some who have the gift of feeling "called", the closest I have come to a "call" is expressed in the opening words of my Masters of Theological Studies thesis in which I explore the experience of hope in my own life.

> Apply your mind to at least one problem which has never been solved, which in general is considered impossible of solution, but which being solved, would help humanity. Do with your life something that has never been done but which you feel needs doing.[13]

I don't have the gift of faith as many have. I do though celebrate the the gift of hope. I have enjoyed more than a decade of formally exploring it and seeing a vision come to be in the form of the Hope

11   Fox, M. (1990). *A Spirituality named Compassion and the Healing of the Global Village, Humpty Dumpty and us*: San Francisco, Harper & Row. p. 31.
12   Fox, M. p. 30.
13   Nininger, H. *Analog Science Fiction and Fact*, Vol. 110, 13, 1990, p. 10.

Foundation of Alberta, now known as Hope Studies Central (University of Alberta). Of the classic virtues of faith, hope and love, hope is clearly the neglected virtue, the least written about, the least understood, and the least studied.

What is this thing called hope?

In 2004 Jaklin Eliott, a delightful Australian colleague, invited me to write the closing chapter of *Interdisciplinary Perspectives on Hope.*[14] In that chapter I point to the complexity of this amazing phenomenon that we call hope: "What is this thing called hope? We ridicule those with too much of it and we hospitalize those with too little. It is dependent on so many things, yet indisputably necessary to most. Those with it live longer, achieve more. Words can destroy it. Science has neglected it. A day without it is horrible. A day with an abundance of it guarantees little." A day with hope guarantees nothing, yet a day without it is despairing.

It was E. De Pressense who said, "We have not learned to suffer without hope."[15] Victor Frankl understood hope as "a spirituality without religion."

Hope has fed my spirit, fueled my passions,

---

14   Jevne, R. (2005). Hope: It's simplicity and complexity, invited chapter for Jaklin Eliott (ed.) (Australia). *Interdisciplinary Perspectives on Hope.* New York, Nova Science Publishers, p.259-289.

15   E. De Pressense. (1868). *The Mystery of Suffering and Other Discourses.* London: Hodder & Stoughton, p.16.

made the impossible seem only improbable. I have never felt without spirit. Passion has come easily whether it was for riding horseback on a Wednesday afternoon when I should have been in home economics class, or helping to establish the only research center in the world that studies hope. I willingly worked extended hours to accomplish what I deemed worthy goals.

There is a good feeling about the footprint, however small, that I have left on the hearts of many people and in the policies of more than one institution. I have seldom felt that I had a restless spirit and often felt a strength of spirit that has to be tempered among those whose presence impedes social equality. It was not always easy to remember that what seems unreasonable or unkind behavior likely had its origin in an unattended wound.

In the process of exploring hope, I began to see the role of suffering in spiritual development. Indeed, a reflection on celebrating spirit would be incomplete without honoring of the place of suffering in our lives. Not uncommonly those people who develop a depth of spirit are those who have experienced or witnessed suffering, whose histories have confronted them with the realities of incapacity, inadequacy, or injustice. CS Lewis in *The Problem with Pain* says, "God whispers to us in our pleasures, speaks in our conscience, but shouts in our pains."[16] It is in

16   Lewis, C. S. (1940). *The Problem with Pain.* Glasgow, Wm. Collins & Co. Ltd, p. 81.

the context of suffering that we are often forged, not only when we are suffering but when we witness suffering. I spoke publicly many times about the life lessons offered by patients suffering from cancer but none are as poignant as the lessons to which we are invited when the suffering is personal.

Sitting in the twilight of my father's hospital room, I wrote:

When Tom died we gasped
When Mom passed
    we ached with the suddenness
With Dad, death will not be so gentle
    in this painful interval between his
    life and death.

Who will I be in this suffering?

Sitting beside his catheter
    reeking with concentrated urine
Crafting the thickened mucus
    in his raw mouth and throat
    onto soft pink sponges and
    learning to call it "mouth care"
Witnessing the droop of his eye
    knowing it bothers him,
    a once handsome man

Attending the wound
> left by the violent retrieval of the tumor
> that haunted us all for the weeks prior.
Advocating and protecting him
> in a system overextended,
> long since corrupted
> by substituting
> technology for compassion.

Who am I in this suffering?

Admiring this man
> grateful and dignified
> in these dark moments
Whispering encouragements
> in the morning twilight
> of his 90th birthday
Knowing the pathology report
> has sealed his death
> before 91.

Who am I in this suffering?

In *The History of Spirit,* Joel Kovel concludes, "We make spirituality; not as we choose, but rather according to the history into which we have been thrown."[17] It is not surprising to me, given the history into which I have been thrown, that I am comfortable

17   Kovel, J. (1991). *History and Spirit: An Inquiry into the Philosophy of Liberation.* Boston: Beacon Press, p.198.

in the Zen tradition. It is easy for me to accept the reality of suffering and impermanence. It feels natural to examine how I deepen my suffering by how I engage in my life circumstance.

For me, the essence of the great traditions resonate commonalities that guide my spirit. Scholars may argue one cannot blend spiritual traditions. However, the love of the Jesus of my upbringing is not so unlike the compassion of the Buddha who recommends the reflection that invites enlightenment. With a lightness of spirit, I suppose my answer to the question of my spirituality is, "I am in my Zen phase!"

I am more interested in obedience to the moment than in accumulating credits for afterlife, more interested in compassion than in judgment. I am more interested in living my spirituality than naming it.

There is an old Hasidic tale that ponders the question, "How can we determine the hour of dawn, when the night ends and the day begins?" The response is, "When you can look into the face of human beings and you have enough light [in you] to recognize them as your brothers and sisters. Up until then, it is night, and darkness is still with us."[18]

18　　　Durback, R. (Ed.). (1989). *Seeds of Hope: A Henri Nouwen Reader*. Toronto: Bantam Books. p. 205.

For Your Reflections

Celebrating Being Human

Unless you go within, you will go without.
Buddhist saying

Tolerance is giving to every other human being
every right that you can claim for yourself.
Robert Ingersol

The hurried, overcommitted way of being in our culture is unhealthy. For many, life is happening at a pace faster than it can be put into perspective. No one seems to being calling "time out" in this game of constant "catch up". Even if we are models of efficiency, life will throw us curves - unsettling, unwelcome, unnerving curves. Without taking time for quiet during the mainstream of our lives, we will find ourselves ill prepared for these disruptive invasions into our planned lives.

In a frenetic world, there is a need for a practice - a personal and private way by which to develop our inner life. There is a need to enter into that quiet place where we can transcend the clutter of life while we clarify issues, arrive at solutions, and develop perspective on the concerns of our lives. A place so quiet, we can cohabit with uncertainty while staying grounded. A place where we are clear about what is truly important. Some of us call it "home". It is an inner home – a place where we feel valued and capable despite the chaos that at times besets us. When we go there, we reconnect with our integrity, our purpose, and our yet undiscovered possibilities. It is a place of acceptance and hope. It is a place of where we can appreciate our humanity.

Celebrating my humanness is not easy on a day when I mumble, stumble, and fumble through the mundane demands of an ordinary day. For someone of my nature, it is not easy to reach the end of the day with a to do list longer than it was in the morning. How can I feel grounded when I lose my cool, lose my keys, and lose my way all on one day? It is not easy to feel good about seemingly unnecessary delays and yet in the culture of technology, delays are the order of the day. No one fixes microwaves any more but it can take you two hours to establish that the warrantee expired last month. The batteries in the smoke detectors provide that "change me, change me" warning tone only on days when I am expecting company momentarily. There is no reason why the garage door opener should stop functioning on the same day that the food processor, my most used gadget, malfunctions. Why does one computer program insist on being reactivated every thirty days despite three technicians having "fixed" the problem?

Waiting is a national pastime. We wait at airports, we wait at stoplights, we wait during road repairs, we wait for repair people, we wait for a human voice after making seven push button selections on a phone, we wait for our tax rebate. We wait to hear if we were successful in a job application. We wait for the results of medical tests. We wait.

The price we pay for the pace and the culture we live in is often hidden. The price is, however, also a function of my attitude, of my ability to be obedient to the moment, to deal with what is rather than what I want. I am not dismissing the destabilizing influence that others contribute by colluding with the presenting disruptions. How do I step aside from the relentless assaults, minor as they are but cumulative in impact and step into a quiet place, a place of reflection where I can attend the often-neglected sphere of hurts and hopes, dreams and dreads, fears and strengths? *Health News* (March 23, 2012) reported that the World Health Organization predicts that by 2020, the prevalence of depression will rival heart desease. There has to be a better way to confront our stress.

The benefits of a positive attitude are now well established. Barbara Fredrickson, a scholar in the field of psychology, provides convincing evidence in *Positivism* that at least a 3/1 ratio of positive to negative feelings and thoughts are necessary for a moderate degree of mental health. She is clear, however, that this doesn't mean dismissing or disguising our authentic negative reactions. It means addressing them. Yet, it is trendy these days to require the positive from our selves.

Barbara Ehrenreich points out in *Bright-sided: How the Relentless Promotion of Positive Thinking Has Undermined America*[19] that there is an unspoken pressure to be positive in mainstream America. She notes that in Calvinist time, to be happy was to be doing wrong. Today, not to be happy is to have failed. Not to be happpy is to commit the sin

---

19   Ehrenreich, B. (2009). *Bright-sided: How the Relentless Pro-motion of Positive Thinking Has Undermined America.* New York: : Metropolitan Books. p. 88.

of discouragement. She defends the right to not be "moonstruck with optimism" and indeed believes that being moonstruck has potentially substantive consequences. I concur. Dismissing our shadow, our dark side is not the answer. Embracing the amazing complexity of our humanness is, in my view, a prerequisite to the health of our inner life.

Some months ago I was asked to prepare a luncheon speech for a fundraiser. The assigned theme was "Being Human". Ironically, the fundraiser never happened but it gave me the opportunity to think intentionally about being human. Part of the text is below.

> I am looking for women (and men) who would like to join me in changing the world – simply by practicing being human and reflecting on your practice of humanness. So many of you are already changing the world, already putting in countless hours as hockey moms, on-call grandparents, board and committee members of countless and important non-profits, more significantly changing lives than you really know. Every time you listen to a friend, every time you provide guidance to a child, every time you encourage or even confront a spouse, every time you are present for a self-conscious teenager, every time you bring a casserole to an ill neighbor, every time you respect the speed limit, every time you reach out to an estranged family member, every time you sit in

silence with a grieving person, you are practicing being human. I am asking you to change the world one person at a time, one action at a time. I am asking you continue to come to know yourself well enough to become the change you want for the world.

I wrestle with what I mean by "being human" and with what I mean by practicing being human. I do know that we all start out in families. Not all families of origin can be described as constructive. Many are unhealthy. As a therapist, I have seen the scars left by abuse and the damage of overindulgence. I have observed the consequences of neglect and the anxiety of wanting to please. In subtle and not so subtle ways, we are taught what it means to be female and what is expected of a male. It is where our inner life, our emotional life is fashioned. Childhood is where our humanness is shaped. With the mind of a child, I discern who I am and who I am supposed to be. With the mind of an adult, I can come to understand it is an amazing journey to the destiny of being fully human. It is a journey we do one day at a time, actually one hour, one moment at a time.

Every time I overcome a fear, every time I learn something new, every time I accept something difficult about myself or someone else, every time I challenge myself to heal from the uncensored, insensitive words or actions of a person who hides their wounds behind hurtful behavior, every time I am willing to forgive, every time I reach out to an estranged relative, or respect their need for distance, every time I come to terms with the reality that I am not assigned to saving the world and yet I am not powerless to help, I am practicing being human.

When I realize that I am not the center of the universe – that my pain, however deep, is a shared pain – a pain shared by every parent who ever lost a child, every spouse who has said a premature goodbye to a life time companion, every athlete whose body could not achieve what her mind could imagine, every business person whose dream evaporated for reasons outside of their control, every home owner who has faced a foreclosure, every elderly citizen who fears aging alone, every street person who could never have envisioned a life of shame – when I understand that we all hurt, I are learning to be human.

When I understand hope is not about having everything turn out okay but about being okay no matter how things turn out, when I am willing to co-habit with uncertainty, when I am willing to honor my journey, when I understand that having no disappointments means I set the bar too low, when I am acquiring wrinkles and being proud of them, when I have stopped apologizing for not being enough, when I have stopped expecting people to be what they are actually not ready to be, when I can laugh at my mistakes and make them fewer times, when I look in the mirror and see a friend, I am growing into my humanness.

When I notice that I have an outside world – a world of commitments, a world of appearances, a world of cell-phones, i-pads, e-mails, meetings and social obligations perpetually inviting me to a frenetic pace driven by an endless to-do list, I am being human. As humans, we are not naturally inclined to attend to our emotional health given the distractions of my culture.

When I notice that I have an inner life – a life of dreams and dreads and mystical experiences, when I notice that I was designed for a whole range of emotions from rage to contentment, from shame to pride, from despair to joy, from boredom to awe, when I notice that feelings change, often for puzzling reasons, when I notice that I am vulnerable and courageous all in one day, when I notice that life is lived by the moment but that I flit often into yesterday and tomorrow, I am being human.

When I notice I have a wishbone, a backbone and a funny bone, I am noticing the anatomy of my inner life skeleton. When I get up in the morning and I want the world to be better because I am in it; when my children feel safe, my partner feels loved and I feel valued I am expanding goodness in my preferred direction. I am though, still human when my tone is impatient, my attention limited, and my expectations unreasonable. When I greet a stranger, when I plug a parking meter simply because I notice it has run out, when I leave a larger than normal tip, when I am curious rather than angry at a rude patron, when I stop blaming others for my choice of emotional response, when I say thank you to the gas attendant, when I send an unexpected card, when I attend a funeral despite a heavy schedule, I am maturing as a human.

When I notice the acorn in each of us that is tomorrow's oak, when I notice how much light a single candle can bring to a cave, when I notice the power of a kind word, and the ripple of a generous gesture, when I notice people can and do change, when I notice courage and replicate it, when I can comment positively on my grandson's career choice even though it was not what I had envisioned for him, when I can be there for my daughter when she is taking the consequences of a poor choice and not say "I told you so" but rather, "You will find your strength and your way, and I will be here for you", when I find the strength to stand for what I value and do so with few words, when I leave judgment at home and respect goes with me everywhere, I am becoming more human.

When a physician sat at my bedside in

Rochester Minnesota at the Mayo clinic in 1978 and said, "We hope we have given you a year" I remember feeling no sense of panic. When at the end of that year I realized I was going to need to pay the bills I had accrued, I set about doing so with gratitude. I was also palpably aware, "This ends. Perhaps not this year, but this ends. This precious thing called life, ends. How do I want to use the life I have been given back?"

Learning to celebrate being human emerged from of falling in love with a prince for thirty-three years who had a heart attack three days after our wedding. Being a public servant and being proud to say so. Being educated by cancer patients. Seeing the fulfillment of the dream of the Hope Foundation, the only one of its kind in the world. Seeing my grandchildren mature into good citizens. Looking into the eyes of my first great grandchild. Being there for my husband during three challenging pilgrimages through the landscape of cancer. Burying my brother, my mother, and my son, all before they were sixty years of age. Journeying with my father to his death at ninety.

Celebrating humanness has meant learning the patience that comes from the rehabilitation required after a head on motor vehicle accident, learning the forgiveness of having my life so abruptly interrupted by someone else's negligence.

It has meant kayaking in a storm in the Baja, facing two to three meter waves as a relative novice, learning to swim a year later. It meant responding to the dare of going to an eight-day silent mediation retreat having never meditated in my life, only to find a deep and powerful quiet that I now continue to nurture.

Becoming human, celebrating being human has meant learning to accept life as both hello and goodbye, recognizing I have made unbelievably naïve, if not stupid decisions, and that I have made remarkably wise choices, replete with suffering and joy. It's an amazing adventure – being human. How do we move to being the person we are meant to be without a raft of revisions and a tyranny of goals?

In this section about the celebrating of being human, three principles form the foundation of moving towards humanness.

First, my inner life is my responsibility. How I use my life is my choice. I have a right to learn by trial and error. I have needed to find out what works for me. No doctrine or ideology, traditional or new age, is a good substitute for sound thinking about my own life. "Follow me and be happy" recipes, no matter how well disguised, are a form of clinging to childhood.

Secondly, I take seriously the realization that I cannot assume to understand someone else. Nor do I assume that I have figured out life. There is so often "a rest of the story". If I know the rest of the story I can be more tolerant of what looks like greed, what is expressed as anger, or what is masked as righteousness. I am not advancing the world with any judgment that lessens another person.

Thirdly, through life experience and thirty years as a therapist, I have come to appreciate the need to stop and think about life. A reflective life takes time but so does repeating the stupid moments of our lives. New tears inform. Tears repeated torment. If life is a series of teachable moments, I prefer new lessons. The process of reflection is a way of calling myself home – to what I value, to what makes sense to me, to what hurts and what delights me.

When I am eighty, I want to feel eighty. I want to have earned the wrinkles, enjoy the peace, and know what my life was about. I want to be endeared to my errors and unrepentant for the adventures that went wrong. The stories I tell will have morsels of wisdom and an abundance of humor. The characters will be complex and their motives, on occasion, still puzzling. Those who read my memoirs will be perplexed at how little of me they knew, and I will delight in them being mystified. What I will have held back will not be a function of shyness, or embarrassment, or any sense of apology for my actions, but a deep sense of not wanting to be a wholly public, transparent person.

I want to have enjoyed noticing my life. Not

wake up at some undesignated age wondering where I have been and what I have been doing for twenty years, unable or unwilling to accept responsibility for what were essentially my choices.

There are many reflective practices. It is ultimately my choice, your choice, based on what works for you. What peace and depth I have I partially attribute to the practice of reflective writing, a way of listening to myself, of being in dialogue with myself. I believe I can change the world by writing – because I can change *my* world by writing. Wouldn't it be amazing, if every person had the opportunity to learn to use a pen, a journal and her/his own companionship to craft a healthy inner life? I have seen it happen with female inmates, with grieving widows, with high needs adolescents.

The activity that I consider to have been my greatest contribution since leaving the university professionally was in response to a request by a friend, an amazing school principal. Together with twenty-three inner city grade eight young women, we did the first ever Junior Pilgrim Writers, an in-residence retreat. Somehow Joan found the funds and made the logistics happen.

A pilgrimage by definition is a journey with both an inner and outer destination embarked upon with an understanding that there will be challenges and that one needs the skills to navigate many landscapes. Students were introduced to writing as a practice that would enable them to deal with their inner landscape which for many of them was a place of pain and turmoil. I had no idea if they would relate to a silver-haired granny who invited them to hours of "noble silence" and expected respect and creativity. During the thirty-six hours that we were together, these young women demonstrated the limitless potential of youth. When they stood in front of me in their Pilgrim Writer golf shirts and bowed their head to receive their Olympic like medal engraved "Pilgrim Writer", I am not sure who was more proud of what they had done in those few hours. Did we reach them all? I don't know. But for each of them who take seriously the care of their inner life, the world for them and others will be better.

For me, silence is imperative to living a life of reflection. Henri Nouwen wrote, "Many people ask me to speak but no one has yet invited me for silence."[20] I cannot sort my life in the midst of the clutter. In *Listening Below the Noise*, Anne Le Claire describes the profound impact of her commitment to one day of silence every two weeks over seventeen years. For me, the choices for silence are less structured and less consistent. Nevertheless, the power of silence has not escaped me. Sometimes I am in grave need of silence long before I actually set aside the assumed barriers to it. In closing the never-delivered speech, I invited participants to:

20   Nouwen, H. (1989). *The Geneses Diary*. New York: Bantam Doubleday. p. 114.

Be just who you are. Don't ask yourself to be more, to stop or to start doing anything. To volunteer more, or less. I am not asking you to drink less coffee, to work out more or to lose or gain weight. I am not asking you to be moonstruck with optimism or even to be more realistically skeptical. Nor am I imploring you to remember more birthdays, or to stop over-consuming. It is your choice to be frustrated with traffic or to stop hurrying. This request doesn't involve revising yourself in any demonstrable or profound way. In fact, experiment with being "obedient to the moment". If you are weary, just be weary. If you are hurrying, just rush. If you are cranky, notice if you take it out on the carrot you are peeling or on your demanding child. If your partner or teenager says something unkind or callous, notice if you can reply, "Oh, that was harsh. You must need a hug", and walk towards them. If you are hurt, notice if you will let a tear come forward.

All I am asking is that you notice. Just notice your life. Notice what feels good and what feels not so good. Notice what happens when you overbook your day with obligation. Notice how you feel when you are caught invited to an uncomfortable social engagement. Notice what happens to you when someone is late. Notice if you notice the strain in your shoulder. Notice if you take time to read. Notice you if care if your cell phone is on. Notice if you apologize or if you never apologize. Notice if you noticed the miracle of a snowflake or the power of our prairie wind. Notice what made you laugh. Notice if you feel the need to turn on the radio or the CD player when you drive. Notice if you sing in the shower or if you need the towels hung straight. Just notice.

For one month, sit, despite your fatigue, at the end of the day, perhaps with a cup of tea, sit in silence and simply recall, or even better, record what you noticed that day. It doesn't need to be an epistle. A list will suffice.

I am asking for a ten-minute commitment. Longer, if you choose. Record it all, without judgment and to the best of your ability, without fail for a month. Let yourself at least review the day. No judgment. Notice what stayed with you. Without judgment is the biggest part of the challenge. Just notice. Record the good, the bad and the ugly. And know that tomorrow might be different. You have that choice. And whatever you notice, whatever you choose, remind yourself that becoming human takes practice.

Celebrating My Place in Life

When you can think of yesterday without regret
and tomorrow without fear,
you are near contentment.

Author unknown

The interplay of fate and choice has brought me to where I am. To a place I call home. Most days, it is easily accessible. Occasionally, it takes some intentionality. Although I love our physical home, its beauty, its quiet, its sense of congruence with who we are, the home I am referring to is the sense of being at home with the person I have become.

In order to claim to have a place in life, I acknowledge that I don't occupy other places. There are paths not taken. I am not sure I consistently took the path less travelled. I did though, recognize some of the intersections as I approached. Others, I only recognize in the rear view mirror.

Might the first six decades have been different? Can I honestly say that I have no regrets? Although none of us can know the consequences of the paths not taken, I am convinced different choices would not have yielded greater life satisfaction.

The obvious 'what might have been' is that I might have been born in another country to different parents, in a different socio-economic strata. I might have spoken another language, held different values, and complied with different traditions. In other words, I might have been a different me. But I was born to good parents in a privileged country.

What if my family had fallen on hard times? What if those times had been hard enough to undermine our dignity, our sense of future, and our sense of hardiness? There were hard times but none that absconded with hope.

I might have had a sister and avoided a lengthy longing for a same sex sibling. Had I had a birth sister I might never have known the gift of Irene's friendship, nor would I have had the humble experience of being chosen as a sister by Sandi and Lynda. Although separated by geography, knowing I have been chosen for what I longed for for many years has quieted a place deep in my inner world. There are other female friends for whom I am very grateful. I now feel I have small network of sisterhood. Had I a natural sister, that might not have happened.

As for careers, I might have been accepted to the mission field when I was nineteen, spent my twenties in Sierra Leon, having learned Swahili before recognizing it was community development, not spiritual development that motivated the application. Whew! Thank goodness I didn't go down that path. Let's not even go there! Perhaps it was divine intervention that prevailed over naivety!

Someone might have told me that when you grow up, you can be a photographer. That it is possible to make a living at what you love to do. But then, given my propensity for risk, I might have been a war correspondent and gotten myself killed. Then again, I might have lived the marginal life that is the destiny of many artists. Then again, I might have been very successful but have had the passion fade.

I might have taken a job in rural community

development and been an adult educator, not plagued with the high-risk patients and chronic exposure to emotional pain and multiple deaths that has been my experience as a psychologist. I would still have written although the subject matter would more likely have been the plight of the rural woman and the demise of the farm family. Perhaps I would have lunched with more politicians and died a slow death of impotency in the world of policymakers.

I might have had much better health. I might have become a high performance athlete. I might not have had to adapt to the unfulfilled dreams that faded with illness and injury. I might never have had to wonder how much more I might have accomplished had I had more consistent health. Yet, had I not been ill, I likely would not have become a health psychologist and experienced the positive domino effect of that choice. Then again, had I had great health, and never felt the shadow of mortality, I might have failed to excel despite vitality to accomplish as much as I have.

With good health, I might have fallen out of one too many canoes, ridden one too many spirited horses, or played one too many games of racquetball. Worst-case scenario, I might have been humbled by accident or illness in irreparable ways. I might have been among the marginalized, groveling for a shoddy room, a second-hand sweater, and a part-time minimum wage job. Somewhere along the line someone, or something, might have closed the doors that led to prosperity. As it was, my interview for a university position began with, "Your references say you are terrific but they also say you may be dying." Not exactly a subtle conversation! I smiled and replied, "I can't deny that I have been ill but I don't smoke, I don't drink, and I don't drive over the speed limit. Is there any point in continuing this interview?" I got the job.

In the realm of relationships, I might have had a child in my first marriage and subsequently never pursued graduate work. I might have been a soccer mom and sat up all night tending a child's chicken pox. Then again, I might have lost that same child in a car accident. Had that child been a male, he might have married me a daughter. Or not. Had my first marriage lasted, I would have lived in Norway. Had that happened, separated by an ocean and most of a continent, I would never have known my own mother as a sister, never seen that I was stolen from her future, never seen in her eyes the pain of the distance that would have separated us daily. Never been there for her at her dramatic early death.

My dad might have predeceased my mom, and I would have had a different place in the heritage of the family farm. She might have lived with us and we might have played together like sisters. She might have been there for the many times I wanted to shop with her, tell her my daily triumphs, celebrate my accolades. I might not have had a kindly father who tried to make up for her early absence.

I might have married my second love and lived by the sea. Walked and talked as we did for eight years. We might have written together; taken the adventures he took alone. Yet, I might have been trapped in a sea of elders, a generation too out of place for my years. I might have ended up yearning for my freedom, hungry to live in my own era. Maybe, maybe not. As it unfolded, we stayed friends until his death.

Had I not married Allen, I might have been without a partner whose daily touch and endless kindness have tended the goodness in me. I might have had the majority of my thirty thousand meals alone in these thirty plus years. I might have had no one with whom to be silly, to share the decisions, to tell stories to or to partake in the greater mystery with me. Without Allen, I would not have had the challenges of being a stepmother and a foster mom, or the joy of being a grandmother.

The grandkids might have lived closer and we would have had memories of them throughout infancy, entering childhood, bursting into adolescence and graduating into adulthood. What we have are a wall full of photographs but few stories we can tell of how these little people discovered their worlds, conquered their fears, pursued their dreams, and grew into the good citizens they have become.

I am at the age where "what might have been"

doesn't feel relevant, doesn't feel emotionally laden with regret or disappointment. What matters now is the place to which I have evolved, the sense that I have made of life to date, the person I want to continue to become. I am much like the character Alice in Robert Fulgrum's book *From Beginning to End,* "Though she was not as thin, attractive, smart, healthy or happy as she might have been, she was thin enough, attractive enough, smart enough, healthy enough and happy enough." And that's an okay place!

My place in life

To name my place in life is to name the organizing principles of my life, what it is that guides my life, that gives me meaning and satisfaction. Although we all have blind spots, to the best of my discernment, I want to live from a place of order in my day to day life, a place of integrity in my inner and professional life, a place of compassion in my relational life, a place of potential relative to my future, and a place called home that is the ground of my existence.

In many ways, I am comfortable with my place in life. I have arrived partially by choice, partially by nature, and partially by circumstance. A place in life is about style. About how I like things to be. About what I work towards. About what I value. It is also about where I choose not to be.

It is easier to discuss what is not my place

in the world. It is not on the cheerleader squad. It is not on the golf course. It is not in the audience. If it requires groveling, I will not be there. If it requires uncomfortable shoes, I am probably not staying long. If there is an abundance of jargon and a wealth of experts professing beatitudes, I am probably yawning or deliberately annoying them before my early exit. If the table talk is of 'new age' remedies for ancient and complex problems, I have probably sent my regrets.

A place of order

At the very day-to-day level, my "place" is tidy and for that I pay dearly! Half of life seems to be putting it away. The dishes, the file folders, the books, the carrot peeler, the client reports, the cheese cutter, the laundry, the computer disks, the photographs, the groceries, the invitations, the CDs, the plane tickets, the specialist's phone number, the Christmas decorations. It never stops. And no one seems to notice.

I am at the age where I want order. I want to know that where I put the peanut butter is where it will be tomorrow. That where the concert tickets are is where I will find them a month from now when I am ready to go out the door. I want everything in my wardrobe to fit and to be color coordinated. I want my books organized so I can find one within a minute of searching for it. I have for years alphabetized my spices and been kidded about it. I like my spices alphabetized! It is so quick to access them. I want a financial accounting of where we are every month or two. I want to know if more is going out than is coming in. I want to know my vehicle is in excellent running condition, that the glove compartment has the insurance slip and registration, and that I can take a guest in my car at any time without wondering if the seats are clear and the floor coverings clean. I still like a hardcopy daybook. I want to look at my book and see what is coming at me. I don't want to open my computer, or some miniature version, use a tiny little pen and poke at things to see if I am free for lunch. I want the shoe polish in an accessible place and I want extra toilet tissue awaiting the need. My grocery list is computerized.

At any given time a hard copy is sitting by the phone, and when I go shopping it is instantly ready to accompany me. There are extra double A batteries in a specific drawer and a place for recycling the old ones. There is a candle with matches in every room. I live in the country and power outages are common. I want an extra set of printer's ink cartridges on hand so I never have to stop and "run to town".

Seven filing cabinets are insufficient for my files. I am not sure what to do about that. I love my darkroom, now digital, because it has a place for everything and everything in its place. I love order and yet, to my knowledge, have never been described as obsessive. Just organized. There was a time when I wasn't organized. Order, I have learned is preferable to chaos and much more aligned with a life of productivity.

A place of integrity

I wrestle to find the words to express what it means to live from a place of integrity. I sense there are three expressions of such intent. The first is what one might called an outer life, the second could be called an inner life, and the third I would call a relationship life.

One night on my way home from doing group therapy, I was stopped by an Royal Canadian Mounted Police officer. Tired, I had inadvertently driven through a small village at eighty kilometers an hour when the speed limit is fifty kilometers per hour. It was at 11:00 pm so fortunately no harm occurred. The officer let me off with a warning not to drive when I am so weary. Little does he know, he forever changed my driving habits. Without knowing quite how, I found myself accepting that I have a responsibility when I drive whether or not there is any immediate danger. I actually, except for rare moments of, choose to obey speed limits. It's not fear. It's not sissy. It is choice.

I celebrate that I am at that age. I am at the age where I simply have little interest in living by someone else's rules and yet, at another level, I am happy to live by a few civil ones that have universal benefit.

It makes ultimate sense to me that we all drive

on the right hand side of the road and that as a society have legislated a safe traveling speed. Speeding is one of the few overt acts of social disobedience to which we turn a blind eye. There are people who defend their right to blatantly disobey the law. Even information about the miniscule advantage of speeding relative to arrival time seems to make no difference to them. They openly deny studies that have demonstrated that self-declared good drivers actually have distorted perceptions of their competence. They remain sure they are the exception. I have yet to see a speed limit sign that says, "Oh, somewhere between 90 and 130 kilometers will be fine!" It puzzles me that the same person who feels he or she is justified in breaking a speed limit will agree that stealing, even a candy bar, isn't right. I wonder how they feel about being honest about their taxes.

Recently, a man driving in the adjacent lane to me was holding a cup of hot coffee in one hand and talking on a cell phone with the other. It made me wonder how was he driving – with his nose? His elbows? Tailgaters defy the realities of physics. Vehicles take a predictable distance to come to a stop. This country has approximately 12,650,000 registered vehicles.[21] We need to honor each other's right to live more than our right to make our own rules.

Whether it is driving regulations, laws to protect the intellectual property of authors, artists

21   Wiki.answers.com/Q/How_many cars are_registered_in_ Canada?

or musicians, complying with recycling policies or completing my tax return honestly, I want to live from a place of integrity. The issue is not whether I agree with each and every detail of our agreement to live together. It is whether I want to live from a place of integrity, to honor the best-to-date efforts of our communities to live together. When no common agreement exists, I hope to make choices with the best interest of others as a consideration equal to my own self-interest. Living from a place of integrity is not solely about living according to the law. Civil obedience is an outward expression of respect for the fact that life if not just about me.

The integrity of an inner life is harder to describe. To live from a place guided by what I have come to value is not always a comfortable or easy place. Sometimes it means going the extra mile when I am weary. Sometimes it means risking being misinterpreted. Sometimes it means agreeing to something towards which I am ambivalent but which requires that I take a stand. Sometimes there is a touch of sadness knowing that the options are limited. Often, it means putting ego aside. Without question, it means taking time to reflect on who and what is important in a given situation. Time for reflection doesn't always feel available. Neglecting the reflective process inevitably has a price. Inner messengers called discontent, frustration, or discouragement will visit to remind me of the inner work I have neglected.

Living from a place of integrity with respect to my inner life also means a deep sense of satisfaction knowing I am where I need to be. It means standing quiet and still in a storm. It means being there for the people who need an anchor in the presence of turmoil or chaos. It means understanding there is a price for what I choose, and that some choices cannot be revisited. Some choices come only once. For me, it also means that I am, in the greater scheme of things, insignificant. I need not overestimate my successes, failures or errors. I want to see in each day, the joy that is there. As Georgia Heard says in *Writing Toward Home*, it can mean "falling in love three times every day". It can mean seeing the miracle in a child's eyes. Savoring a new recipe. Touching a wounded bird. Reaching out in a moment of suffering. Being right with myself in each of those moments.

Integrity in relationships, the third domain, is the place where inner meets outer. Let's take the professional relationship out of this discussion and talk about my personal exchanges. I am at the age where I don't want to tip toe. I am at that age where I no longer want to held hostage to the whims or needs of someone's pathology. The problem is that I sometimes don't want to tolerate aspects of others' lives that impinge on my freedoms, even in a minor way. I don't want you to have needs that mean I have to work at connecting with you. Yet, I know this is my work, as a person and, in my case, as a professional.

To live with integrity is to do my best to transcend my annoyances and respect you. I don't always do it well.

At a personal level, I would prefer that if two friends don't relate well to each other together that they sort it out themselves. I don't want to be part of the dance. If you ask me a question, expect a straight answer. If you tell me a secret, expect I will keep it (unless you are telling me you will harm yourself or someone else or that you have abused a child). As a therapist, I have been keeping secrets for years. They are gifts of trust.

If you need something from me, come out and ask. If I can provide it, I will willingly respond. If I can't, I will say so and try to find another way to be supportive. If you have food allergies, I am happy to cook a special meal. Just don't whine.

If you believe you need to wear a suit to be competent, wear your suit. Just don't ask me to be a creative thinker with a nylon grotto around my waist and a bra cutting through my chest. As for uncomfortable shoes, they were gone two decades ago. I am at that age the comfort of my shoes is more important than whether I am in the latest profession uniform. At forty, I stopped wearing uncomfortable shoes. At fifty, I said goodbye to "suits". At sixty, it was time to don gracious simplicity accented with a natural complexion and a classy no effort hairstyle.

I am at the age where people who cling to the victim role are not easy for me. Having been a therapist for years, I am used to witnessing the courage of clients. Most clients want to live life differently, not stay meeting their needs by being needy. They come to the realization that if they want something different in their life, they will need to do something different with their life. Many remarkable people I think of might well have justified remaining victims of circumstances beyond their control. Most of us can and want to help people on their way to being remarkable, whether that is a mom raising four little ones alone, whether it is a soldier adjusting to an amputation, whether it is a businessperson adapting to a huge change in the marketplace. All of us could use with a little pampering at times. If you need pampering, I can do that. You don't have to be a victim to be pampered by me.

If you set a deadline, meet it, or tell me that you can't. Don't pretend you are on the verge of meeting it. If you are prone to guilt, don't expect me to share it or to worry about yours. If you have sadness, I will put on the teapot and listen and say little. I don't mind you bragging. There is little enough room for applauding our successes. Go ahead and outright brag, only though about what you have actually done.

There is something about people who speak of their successes in inflated ways that gives them away. Genuine achievement somehow has a ring of genuine pride. I loved a young woman who called me on her cell phone having just left a conference room where she had given her first public presentation. The energy in her voice regenerated me for the day. Those moments need to be shared. We need to cheer for each other.

Maturity doesn't mean we lose our exuberance, that everything has to be cool and calm. Forget cool and calm. If you belly laugh, belly laugh. Don't sniffle into a Kleenex.

A client endeared herself to me when she learned my dog died. Molly used to greet her, tail wagging every session. Her tears were a statement of genuinely missing, not only for Molly but also for whatever she had lost over the years. As well, it was the gift of permission to cry when your dog dies. That's not pathology. That's humanness.

My place in life is to ask more questions, share fewer answers. To walk slower and more deliberately. To scratch the dog's head more often. To meditate as I prepare food. To eat dessert first. To speak my piece, more accurately to speak my peace. To never for the sake of social grace or civility forsake my truth yet, at the same time, to be compassionate about my shortcomings and those of others.

In my professional life, living from a place of integrity has taken time. I had to find my professional self and my professional place. I never felt I had a pre-destined place, unlike my friend Donna, who always knew she would be a nun. Or my friend Janet, whose musical talent predestined her fate. The search for meaning whispered throughout my teenage years and into my twenties. I kept saying as Stephen Crane did in his poem, *A man said to the universe* "I exist" and the Universe echoed in return, "That fact has not created in me a sense of obligation."

I assumed that I would find a place, personally or professionally, but then inevitably I would move on. Circumstance or choice would necessitate crafting a new place. For years, I looked for a "professional home". Am I teacher? A counselor? When I became a psychologist, the questions changed only slightly. Was I a cognitivist? A Rogerian? A whatever? With experience I came to understand that I was the instrument, not the theory. In recent years, there is more than adequate research to defend that position. The integrity is in me, not in a theory or in a technique. Less than ten per cent of therapeutic outcome of counseling is attributed to the underlying theory of treatment. We now know that the client/therapist alliance, as we call it, is central to the helping process. I am reminded of the participant in a 1950 conference who, only partially facetiously said, "Psychotherapy is an undefined technique applied to unspecified problems with unpredictable outcomes. For this technique, we recommend rigorous training."[22]

Early in my development as a professional, I thought of that statement as a justifiable license for the untrained to enter the arena of human suffering.

22   Arkowitz, H. & Lilienfeld, S. (2006). Psychotherapy on Trial. *Scientific American Mind* 17, 41-48. p. 44.

Now I understand it differently. I now want to see the evidence. If I am being asked for $1000.00 for a weekend workshop, or $40.00 for a DVD, there ought to be information supporting the credibility of the approach and the integrity of the promoter.

I am increasingly concerned about short cut recipes to healing emotional suffering offered by self-appointed, uneducated, often well-intentioned gurus. "Client Beware" is my advice. Psychology is not devoid of its own fads and opportunists. It isn't hard to find something that will make you feel better for a short period of time. Hopefully, the Visa bill for the brief miracle cure was worthwhile. I have seen psychological fads come and go, and I have witnessed the trail of damage left in their wake. When the halo effect fades, you are of course, responsible for sustaining the placebo effects. The corporate demands of insurance plans are influencing practice. Not uncommonly what has plagued someone for decades is allocated six sessions for cure. Mental health has become a commodity.

From a place of professional integrity, I can, for the most part, stand firmly and quietly in the storms of others. I can be a beacon to usher them to a safe cove. I am able to offer solace and strength as they pull into harbor to repair their sail and prepare to navigate again.

The place of professional integrity is a place of deep respect – a deep respect for being trusted to use myself and my skills in the context of others' suffering, a deep respect for my belief that people must become students of their own lives and therapists of their own souls. There is rarely a magical transformation. There is no "new self-potion". Maturity is rarely easily earned and rarely easily sustained initially. When reconstructing self, it is useful to know the credentials and integrity of the person you choose to work with. No therapist is a match for every client. However, I have been known to say, "We don't pay a pilot for those fair weather flights. We pay them to land in the Hudson River. And even then a crash is a possibility." Helping people navigate the storms and darkness of their lives is a sacred trust.

A place of compassion

In the professional domain, compassion is the core of my discipline. To live from a place of integrity in relationships is perhaps life's greatest challenge. It requires navigating the readiness on my inner life and the readiness of the 'other', finding a balance between compassion and directness.

In our personal lives being unkind, being demanding, being threatening - may generate obedience but it does little to build bridges or open dialogue. Almost equally destructive is indifference. Compassion may be much slower to influence than threat. Compassion though is not passive. It demands that I see the person before me as my equal even if we have major differences. It demands that I not, as the younger generation says, 'wimp out' and forgo any expectations in relationships. It requires that I know what I value, what I stand for and yet not be coercive. It means that I not use sheer power to overcome another. Tough order. I hold to it as a useful aspiration even if I fall short of consistent compliance.

I am at that age where I don't want to be part of putting distance between us as people, except in vehicles, whether that is within my family, in a work setting, between offenders and the community, between the ill and the well. We are all just one flaw, one accident, or one twist of fate from being the "other" who is disadvantaged, physically or spiritually.

I am at that age where I don't want to use energy for confrontation. Not that I ever did. It takes energy to confront and energy not to confront. I don't want either. I just want you to be you, and me to be me. And if we can, let's have tea together to see if we can deepen our understanding of each other.

Disrespect and entitlement injure. They hurt people. Callous and unkind remarks of any nature seldom improve a situation. Humor is too thin a veil to disguise essentially offensive material. What would happen if for one day we experimented with radical acceptance? Instead of being "right", instead of defending our own positions, we can choose to become inquirers, curious about how others arrived at their opinions, particularly when we feel we obviously hold the correct view.

And yet, I am at that age, if indeed it is age related, where I accept respect can't be legislated. I don't resist legislation on the basis of infringement of rights. I am though aware that human nature doesn't necessarily respond to logic. I recognize though that many transitions have been furthered by legal consequences being attached to behavior. Perhaps one forerunner of compassion is the establishing of codes of conduct for which there are consequences.

A place of potential

I never want to stop learning. I never want to stop having new experiences. I keep a bucket list equal to my age so it actually grows every year. I celebrate the ability to keep learning. I deeply respect and take joy in the fact that at seventy-five Allen decided he would return to university for his third degree. This time in philosophy. I love the discussions that his readings brought to our relationship. If I knew where to apply, I would get an extension on life with a guarantee or at least a warranty on health so I could keep learning.

Throughout my life I have yearned for stability and craved adventure. That's a bind at times. Given the former, until recently, I was always employed. Being in public service was very congruent with my values. My version of adventure in my young adulthood amounted to tying the zipper of the tent flap to the one shoe I would wear at nights as I traveled the west coast alone in my 1966 pink Pontiac Parisienne. I was convinced by so doing that any intruder would awaken me. What didn't seem to occur to me is that I might be at a disadvantage to flee given that I was tied to the tent! I am not giving up adventure! I may though need to redefine it.

From where I stand, I still want adventure. Maybe even serious physical adventure. Kayaking in the Baja was awesome several years ago. I am keeping my eye out for something that is possible, given my circumstance. Some form of secular pilgrimage is appealing but has not yet taken shape.

I no longer live near fear. I no longer pull into the harbour of regret. For the most part, I walk the path of gracious aging. I don't have the energy to rage about it. I live in a rhythm of fatigue and energy constantly repairing this or that, nurturing any number of bodily parts that are prematurely malfunctioning. I remain committed to doing what is within my control. Perhaps someday, I will fulfill my dream of a dog sled trip across northern Sweden. I often, not always, swim my forty laps twice weekly relatively consistently in response to the truth of "use it or lose it."

At this intersection in life, I have to make choices about how to use my time. I don't wish to be one of those retirees whose badge of honor is being able to say, "I am busier than I ever was". Then why retire? I am happy to do many errands or favors, happy

I now have the time to offer that which once was not an option. Just say "thank you." Don't presume I am standing around waiting for meaning in my life and serving you does it. At one level, it does. At another level, I don't care to be anyone's unwilling servant. It is fun to be able to stand in where I could not for years. My willingness to do so will be tempered by reciprocity and by a simple thank you, or its absence. I continue to work part time and my life has purpose. I want to use much of my time deepening and expressing that purpose.

As I look from the short end of the life line, I know there is much less time left than has passed, and I don't want to spend many hours of it listening to trivia. Belly laughs, yes. So what would trivia be? That would be the endless chatter about grandchildren, the latest who is best at something competition on television or the quality of the putting greens at golf courses where you paid exorbitant fees. I simply don't care. Indeed, that makes it more difficult to have an extended conversation. I do know if we avoid those topics, we will find one of much more substance. Your hobby. Mine. The latest medical breakthrough. A good book. What we are learning. What is concerning us in the context of our families or communities. Something. Just bless me now and let me escape conversation driven by social graces.

More and more my place is on the acreage. Hosting the wounded, pampering friends, savoring the solitude. I want to be in an artist's place. Nipping buds off roses, moving lady bugs off plants to avoid the dose of weed killer, walking Molly, baking oatmeal cookies, sharing afternoons with would be photographers, writing short and long pieces about our inner lives. Feeding my soul with gentleness and my body with homegrown herbs. Hopefully more of these activities are awaiting my future.

A place called "in between"

I have lived 'in between' often. In between health and illness. In between relationships. In between introversion and extroversion. In between the secular and the sacred. In between competence and fear of failure. "In between" is at the center of neither and on the fringe of both.

I am between employed and retired. Metaphorically, my place has been on the ball diamond. I used to be a great short stop. At one time, I was captain. Now my place is to coach. Soon it will be to sit in the bleachers and yell, "Go kids Go". Later, I will sip tea and ask how the game is going.

There are times when I still feel the place I occupy is an intersection. I am directing traffic. Everyone is going somewhere, even if they are lost. With my direction, people are finding their way to medical help, to emotional balance, to graduate degrees, to a love of photography, and to confidence in writing. It feels though that my shift relief has gotten lost, and I am destined to die on my feet in the interim. Others are whizzing by on their way to this or that, unaware of how they endanger all of us. Thankfully that time is passing. The traffic is slowing, and I direct only at peak hours and during emergencies.

I am between freedom and obligation. On the cusp of sufficient resources, I can generate sufficient income to meet our present needs with only part time work. My need to influence is slipping quickly into the desire for flexibility, an extra hour's rest, and solitude for creative activity. Until then, I will live the freedom of choice as I balance my vision with my energy. I yearn for the freedom to live without a 'to do' list, and the first thing I shall do upon full retirement is remove my wristwatch.

A place called home

The one place where I am unequivocally sure I belong is beside Allen. For over thirty years, I have had a place on his arm at social events, at his bedside in medical crises, in his decision-making on our behalf, as his companion on travels, and irrefutably deep in his open and loving heart. My place is to grow old on the same pillow and to imagine together that we shall never part.

Epilogue

Inevitably fate deflected my dream.
On September 8, 2013,
after a shared journey of deep and quiet
courage with Allen, I was left to forge
a new future alone.

Little did I imagine that life would provide much
more to celebrate before my own parting.

For further information about Dr. Ronna Jevne
and her work contact:
ronnajevne.ca.

For information about Prairie Wind Writing Centre
Contact:
prairiewindwriting@gmail.com

Published Works

Authored

Celebrating 60: Impulsive meditations on six decades.

Hope in practice: Selected conversations. (Editor)

Hoping, coping, and moping: Handling life when illness makes it tough.

It all begins with hope: Patients, caregivers and the bereaved speak out.

Living Life as a Writer: Getting to know your inner author.

Louis' Path.

Tea for the Inner Me: Blending tea with reflection.

Voice of hope: Heard across the heart of life.

Zen and the Art of Illness: Surrendering to the Moment.

Published Works

Co-authored

Finding hope: Seeing the world in a brighter light. With J. Miller

Images and Echoes: Exploring your life with photography and writing. (Editor)

No time for nonsense: Self-help for the seriously ill. With A. Levitan

Striving for health: Living with broken dreams. With H. Zingle

When dreams don't work: Professional caregivers and burnout. With D. Williamson

The Hope Journal: With J. Gurnett

About the Author

Ronna Fay Jevne

Ronna Jevne is a professor emeritus of the University of Alberta. Her career has spanned decades as a teacher, psychologist, professor, inspirational speaker, and the author of more than a dozen books.

She shares her love of writing, particularly reflective writing with students, patients, health care professionals, high needs adolescents, inmates, correctional officers, and many others who enjoy the benefits of writing to enhance well-being.

Ronna lives in a quiet rural setting with her husband, Hal and their red heeler, Spirit.

Ronna and Hal share their commitment to writing through the Prairie Wind Writing Centre.

prairiewindwritingcentre.ca